RULES
FOR
RADICALS

RULES
FOR
RADICALS

*A Practical Primer
for Realistic Radicals*

SAUL D. ALINSKY

VINTAGE BOOKS
A Division of Random House/New York

PERSONAL ACKNOWLEDGMENTS

To Jason Epstein for his prodding, patience and understanding, and for being a beautiful editor.
To Cicely Nichols for the hours of painstaking editorial assistance.
To Susan Rabiner for being the shock absorber between the corporate structure of Random House and this writer.
To Georgia Harper my heartfelt gratitude for the months of typing and typing and for staying with me through the years of getting this book together.

To Irene

"Where there are no men, be thou a man."

—RABBI HILLEL

"Let them call me rebel and welcome, I feel no concern from it; but I should suffer the misery of devils, were I to make a whore of my soul . . ."

—THOMAS PAINE

Lest we forget at least an over-the-shoulder acknowledgment to the very first radical: from all our legends, mythology, and history (and who is to know where mythology leaves off and history begins— or which is which), the first radical known to man who rebelled against the establishment and did it so effectively that he at least won his own kingdom —Lucifer.

—SAUL ALINSKY

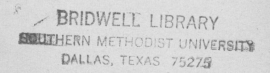

Contents

Prologue

THE REVOLUTIONARY FORCE today has two targets, moral as well as material. Its young protagonists are one moment reminiscent of the idealistic early Christians, yet they also urge violence and cry, "Burn the system down!" They have no illusions about the system, but plenty of illusions about the way to change our world. It is to this point that I have written this book. These words are written in desperation, partly because it is what they do and will do that will give meaning to what I and the radicals of my generation have done with our lives.

They are now the vanguard, and they had to start almost from scratch. Few of us survived the Joe McCarthy holocaust of the early 1950s and of those there were even fewer whose understanding and insights had developed beyond the dialectical materialism of orthodox Marxism. My fellow radicals who were supposed to pass on the torch of experience and insights to a new genera-

tion just were not there. As the young looked at the society
around them, it was all, in their words, "materialistic,
decadent, bourgeois in its values, bankrupt and violent."
Is it any wonder that they rejected us in toto.

Today's generation is desperately trying to make some
sense out of their lives and out of the world. Most of them
are products of the middle class. They have rejected their
materialistic backgrounds, the goal of a well-paid job, suburban home, automobile, country club membership, first-
class travel, status, security, and everything that meant
success to their parents. They have had it. They watched
it lead their parents to tranquilizers, alcohol, long-term-
endurance marriages, or divorces, high blood pressure,
ulcers, frustration, and the disillusionment of "the good
life." They have seen the almost unbelievable idiocy of
our political leadership—in the past political leaders, rang-
ing from the mayors to governors to the White House,
were regarded with respect and almost reverence; today
they are viewed with contempt. This negativism now
extends to all institutions, from the police and the courts
to "the system" itself. We are living in a world of mass
media which daily exposes society's innate hypocrisy, its
contradictions and the apparent failure of almost every
facet of our social and political life. The young have seen
their "activist" participatory democracy turn into its antithesis—nihilistic bombing and murder. The political
panaceas of the past, such as the revolutions in Russia and
China, have become the same old stuff under a different
name. The search for freedom does not seem to have any
road or destination. The young are inundated with a bar-
rage of information and facts so overwhelming that the
world has come to seem an utter bedlam, which has them
spinning in a frenzy, looking for what man has always

looked for from the beginning of time, a way of life that has some meaning or sense. A way of life means a certain degree of order where things have some relationship and can be pieced together into a system that at least provides some clues to what life is about. Men have always yearned for and sought direction by setting up religions, inventing political philosophies, creating scientific systems like Newton's, or formulating ideologies of various kinds. This is what is behind the common cliché, "getting it all together" —despite the realization that all values and factors are relative, fluid, and changing, and that it will be possible to "get it all together" only relatively. The elements will shift and move together just like the changing pattern in a turning kaleidoscope.

In the past the "world," whether in its physical or intellectual terms, was much smaller, simpler, and more orderly. It inspired credibility. Today everything is so complex as to be incomprehensible. What sense does it make for men to walk on the moon while other men are waiting on welfare lines, or in Vietnam killing and dying for a corrupt dictatorship in the name of freedom? These are the days when man has his hands on the sublime while he is up to his hips in the muck of madness. The establishment in many ways is as suicidal as some of the far left, except that they are infinitely more destructive than the far left can ever be. The outcome of the hopelessness and despair is morbidity. There is a feeling of death hanging over the nation.

Today's generation faces all this and says, "I don't want to spend my life the way my family and their friends have. I want to do something, to create, to be me, to 'do my own thing,' to live. The older generation doesn't understand and worse doesn't want to. I don't want to be just a piece of data to be fed into a computer or a statistic in a public opinion poll, just a voter carrying a credit card." To the young the world seems insane and falling apart.

On the other side is the older generation, whose members are no less confused. If they are not as vocal or conscious, it may be because they can escape to a past when the world was simpler. They can still cling to the old values in the simple hope that everything will work out somehow, some way. That the younger generation will "straighten out" with the passing of time. Unable to come to grips with the world as it is, they retreat in any confrontation with the younger generation with that infuriating cliché, *"when you get older you'll understand."* One wonders at their reaction if some youngster were to reply, *"When you get younger* which will never be *then you'll understand,* so of course you'll never understand." Those of the older generation who claim a desire to understand say, "When I talk to my kids or their friends I'll say to them, 'Look, I believe what you have to tell me is important and I respect it. You call me a square and say that 'I'm not with it' or 'I don't know where it's at' or 'I don't know where the scene is' and all of the rest of the words you use. Well, I'm going to agree with you. So suppose you tell me. What do you want? What do you mean when you say 'I want to do my thing.' What the hell is your thing? You say you want a better world. Like what? And don't tell me a world of peace and love and all the rest of that stuff because people are people, as you will find out when you get older—I'm sorry, I didn't mean to say anything about 'when you get older.' I really do respect what you have to say. Now why don't you answer me? Do you know what you want? Do you know what you're talking about? Why can't we get together?' "

And that is what we call the generation gap.

What the present generation wants is what all generations have always wanted—a meaning, a sense of what the world and life are—a chance to strive for some sort of order.

If the young were now writing our Declaration of Independence they would begin, "When in the course of inhuman events . . ." and their bill of particulars would range from Vietnam to our black, Chicano, and Puerto Rican ghettos, to the migrant workers, to Appalachia, to the hate, ignorance, disease, and starvation in the world. Such a bill of particulars would emphasize the absurdity of human affairs and the forlornness and emptiness, the fearful loneliness that comes from not knowing if there is any meaning to our lives.

When they talk of values they're asking for a reason. They are searching for an answer, at least for a time, to man's greatest question, "Why am I here?"

The young react to their chaotic world in different ways. Some panic and run, rationalizing that the system is going to collapse anyway of its own rot and corruption and so they're copping out, going hippie or yippie, taking drugs, trying communes, anything to escape. Others went for pointless sure-loser confrontations so that they could fortify their rationalization and say, "Well, we tried and did our part" and then they copped out too. Others sick with guilt and not knowing where to turn or what to do went berserk. These were the Weathermen and their like: they took the grand cop-out, suicide. To these I have nothing to say or give but pity—and in some cases contempt, for such as those who leave their dead comrades and take off for Algeria or other points.

What I have to say in this book is not the arrogance

of unsolicited advice. It is the experience and counsel that so many young people have questioned me about through all-night sessions on hundreds of campuses in America. It is for those young radicals who are committed to the fight, committed to life.

Remember we are talking about revolution, not revelation; you can miss the target by shooting too high as well as too low. First, there are no rules for revolution any more than there are rules for love or rules for happiness, *but* there are rules for radicals who want to change their world; there are certain central concepts of action in human politics that operate regardless of the scene or the time. To know these is basic to a pragmatic attack on the system. These rules make the difference between being a realistic radical and being a rhetorical one who uses the tired old words and slogans, calls the police "pig" or "white fascist racist" or "motherfucker" and has so stereotyped himself that others react by saying, "Oh, he's one of those," and then promptly turn off.

This failure of many of our younger activists to understand the art of communication has been disastrous. Even the most elementary grasp of the fundamental idea that one communicates within the experience of his audience— and gives full respect to the other's values—would have ruled out attacks on the American flag. The responsible organizer would have known that it is the establishment that has betrayed the flag while the flag, itself, remains the glorious symbol of America's hopes and aspirations, and he would have conveyed this message to his audience. On another level of communication, humor is essential, for through humor much is accepted that would have been rejected if presented seriously. This is a sad and lonely generation. It laughs too little, and this, too, is tragic.

For the real radical, doing "his thing" is to do the social thing, for and with people. In a world where everything is so interrelated that one feels helpless to know where or how to grab hold and act, defeat sets in; for years there have been people who've found society too overwhelming and have withdrawn, concentrated on "doing their own thing." Generally we have put them into mental hospitals and diagnosed them as schizophrenics. If the real radical finds that having long hair sets up psychological barriers to communication and organization, he cuts his hair. If I were organizing in an orthodox Jewish community I would not walk in there eating a ham sandwich, unless I wanted to be rejected so I could have an excuse to cop out. My "thing," if I want to organize, is solid communication with the people in the community. Lacking communication I am in reality silent; throughout history silence has been regarded as assent—in this case assent to the system.

As an organizer I start from where the world is, as it is, not as I would like it to be. That we accept the world as it is does not in any sense weaken our desire to change it into what we believe it should be—it is necessary to begin where the world is if we are going to change it to what we think it should be. That means working in the system.

There's another reason for working inside the system. Dostoevski said that taking a new step is what people fear most. Any revolutionary change must be preceded by a passive, affirmative, non-challenging attitude toward change among the mass of our people. They must feel so frustrated, so defeated, so lost, so futureless in the prevailing system that they are willing to let go of the past and chance the future. This acceptance is the reformation essential to any revolution. To bring on this reformation re-

quires that the organizer work inside the system, among
not only the middle class but the 40 per cent of American
families—more than seventy million people—whose incomes range from $5,000 to $10,000 a year. They cannot be
dismissed by labeling them blue collar or hard hat. They
will not continue to be relatively passive and slightly challenging. If we fail to communicate with them, if we don't
encourage them to form alliances with us, they will move
to the right. Maybe they will anyway, but let's not let it
happen by default.

Our youth are impatient with the preliminaries that
are essential to purposeful action. Effective organization is
thwarted by the desire for instant and dramatic change, or
as I have phrased it elsewhere the demand for revelation
rather than revolution. It's the kind of thing we see in play
writing; the first act introduces the characters and the plot,
in the second act the plot and characters are developed as
the play strives to hold the audience's attention. In the
final act good and evil have their dramatic confrontation
and resolution. The present generation wants to go right
into the third act, skipping the first two, in which case
there is no play, nothing but confrontation for confrontation's sake—a flare-up and back to darkness. To build a
powerful organization takes time. It is tedious, but that's
the way the game is played—if you want to play and not
just yell, "Kill the umpire."

What is the alternative to working "inside" the system? A mess of rhetorical garbage about "Burn the system
down!" Yippie yells of "Do it!" or "Do your thing." What
else? Bombs? Sniping? Silence when police are killed and
screams of "murdering fascist pigs" when others are killed?
Attacking and baiting the police? Public suicide? "Power
comes out of the barrel of a gun!" is an absurd rallying cry

when the other side has all the guns. Lenin was a pragmatist; when he returned to what was then Petrograd from exile, he said that the Bolsheviks stood for getting power through the ballot but would reconsider after they got the guns! Militant mouthings? Spouting quotes from Mao, Castro, and Che Guevara, which are as germane to our highly technological, computerized, cybernetic, nuclear-powered, mass media society as a stagecoach on a jet runway at Kennedy airport?

Let us in the name of radical pragmatism not forget that in our system with all its repressions we can still speak out and denounce the administration, attack its policies, work to build an opposition political base. True, there is government harassment, but there still is that relative freedom to fight. I can attack my government, try to organize to change it. That's more than I can do in Moscow, Peking, or Havana. Remember the reaction of the Red Guard to the "cultural revolution" and the fate of the Chinese college students. Just a few of the violent episodes of bombings or a courtroom shootout that we have experienced here would have resulted in a sweeping purge and mass executions in Russia, China, or Cuba. Let's keep some perspective.

We will start with the system because there is no other place to start from except political lunacy. It is most important for those of us who want revolutionary change to understand that revolution must be preceded by reformation. To assume that a political revolution can survive without the supporting base of a popular reformation is to ask for the impossible in politics.

Men don't like to step abruptly out of the security of familiar experience; they need a bridge to cross from their own experience to a new way. A revolutionary organizer

must shake up the prevailing patterns of their lives—
agitate, create disenchantment and discontent with the
current values, to produce, if not a passion for change, at
least a passive, affirmative, non-challenging climate.

"The Revolution was effected before the war com-
menced," John Adams wrote. "The Revolution was in the
hearts and minds of the people . . . This radical change in
the principles, opinions, sentiments and affections of the
people was the real American Revolution." A revolution
without a prior reformation would collapse or become a
totalitarian tyranny.

A reformation means that masses of our people have
reached the point of disillusionment with past ways and
values. They don't know what will work but they do know
that the prevailing system is self-defeating, frustrating,
and hopeless. They won't act for change but won't strongly
oppose those who do. The time is then ripe for revolution.

Those who, for whatever combination of reasons, encourage the opposite of reformation, become the unwitting
allies of the far political right. Parts of the far left have
gone so far in the political circle that they are now all but
indistinguishable from the extreme right. It reminds me of
the days when Hitler, new on the scene, was excused for
his actions by "humanitarians" on the grounds of a paternal
rejection and childhood trauma. When there are people
who espouse the assassination of Senator Robert Kennedy
or the Tate murders or the Marin County Courthouse kidnapping and killings or the University of Wisconsin bombing and killing as "revolutionary acts," then we are dealing
with people who are merely hiding psychosis behind a political mask. The masses of people recoil with horror and
say, "Our way is bad and we were willing to let it change,
but certainly not for this murderous madness—no matter

how bad things are now, they are better than that." So they
begin to turn back. They regress into acceptance of a coming massive repression in the name of "law and order."

In the midst of the gassing and violence by the Chicago Police and National Guard during the 1968 Democratic Convention many students asked me, "Do you still
believe we should try to work inside our system?"

These were students who had been with Eugene
McCarthy in New Hampshire and followed him across the
country. Some had been with Robert Kennedy when he
was killed in Los Angeles. Many of the tears that were
shed in Chicago were not from gas. "Mr. Alinsky, we
fought in primary after primary and the people voted *no*
on Vietnam. Look at that convention. They're not paying
any attention to the vote. Look at your police and the
army. You still want us to work in the system?"

It hurt me to see the American army with drawn
bayonets advancing on American boys and girls. But the
answer I gave the young radicals seemed to me the only
realistic one: "Do one of three things. One, go find a wail-
ing wall and feel sorry for yourselves. Two, go psycho and
start bombing—but this will only swing people to the
right. Three, learn a lesson. Go home, organize, build
power and at the next convention, *you be the delegates.*"

Remember: once you organize people around something as commonly agreed upon as pollution, then an organized people is on the move. From there it's a short and
natural step to political pollution, to Pentagon pollution.

It is not enough just to elect your candidates. You
must keep the pressure on. Radicals should keep in mind
Franklin D. Roosevelt's response to a reform delegation,
"Okay, you've convinced me. Now go on out and bring
pressure on me!" Action comes from keeping the heat on.

No politician can sit on a hot issue if you make it hot enough.

As for Vietnam, I would like to see our nation be the first in the history of man to publicly say, "We were wrong! What we did was horrible. We got in and kept getting in deeper and deeper and at every step we invented new reasons for staying. We have paid part of the price in 44,000 dead Americans. There is nothing we can ever do to make it up to the people of Indo-China—or to our own people—but we will try. We believe that our world has come of age so that it is no longer a sign of weakness or defeat to abandon a childish pride and vanity, to admit we were wrong." Such an admission would shake up the foreign policy concepts of all nations and open the door to a new international order. This is our alternative to Vietnam—anything else is the old makeshift patchwork. If this were to happen, Vietnam may even have been somewhat worth it.

A final word on our system. The democratic ideal springs from the ideas of liberty, equality, majority rule through free elections, protection of the rights of minorities, and freedom to subscribe to multiple loyalties in matters of religion, economics, and politics rather than to a total loyalty to the state. The spirit of democracy is the idea of importance and worth in the individual, and faith in the kind of world where the individual can achieve as much of his potential as possible.

Great dangers always accompany great opportunities. The possibility of destruction is always implicit in the act of creation. Thus the greatest enemy of individual freedom is the individual himself.

From the beginning the weakness as well as the strength of the democratic ideal has been the people.

People cannot be free unless they are willing to sacrifice some of their interests to guarantee the freedom of others. The price of democracy is the ongoing pursuit of the common good by *all* of the people. One hundred and thirty-five years ago Tocqueville* gravely warned that unless individual citizens were regularly involved in the action of governing themselves, self-government would pass from the scene. Citizen participation is the animating spirit and force in a society predicated on voluntarism.

We are not here concerned with people who profess the democratic faith but yearn for the dark security of dependency where they can be spared the burden of decisions. Reluctant to grow up, or incapable of doing so, they want to remain children and be cared for by others. Those who can, should be encouraged to grow; for the others, the fault lies not in the system but in themselves.

Here we are desperately concerned with the vast mass of our people who, thwarted through lack of interest or opportunity, or both, do not participate in the endless re-

---

* "It must not be forgotten that it is especially dangerous to enslave men in the minor details of life. For my own part, I should be inclined to think freedom less necessary in great things than in little ones, if it were possible to be secure of the one without possessing the other.

"Subjection in minor affairs breaks out every day, and is felt by the whole community indiscriminately. It does not drive men to resistance, but it crosses them at every turn, till they are led to surrender the exercise of their will. Thus their spirit is gradually broken and their character enervated; whereas that obedience, which is exacted on a few important but rare occasions, only exhibits servitude at certain intervals, and throws the burden of it upon a small number of men. It is vain to summon a people, which has been rendered so dependent on the central power, to choose from time to time the representatives of that power; this rare and brief exercise of their free choice, however, important it may be, will not prevent them from gradually losing the faculties of thinking, feeling, and acting for themselves, and thus gradually falling below the level of humanity."

—Alexis de Tocqueville, *Democracy in America*

sponsibilities of citizenship and are resigned to lives determined by others. To lose your "identity" as a citizen of democracy is but a step from losing your identity as a person. People react to this frustration by not acting at all. The separation of the people from the routine daily functions of citizenship is heartbreak in a democracy.

It is a grave situation when a people resign their citizenship or when a resident of a great city, though he may desire to take a hand, lacks the means to participate. That citizen sinks further into apathy, anonymity, and depersonalization. The result is that he comes to depend on public authority and a state of civic-sclerosis sets in.

From time to time there have been external enemies at our gates; there has always been the enemy within, the hidden and malignant inertia that foreshadows more certain destruction to our life and future than any nuclear warhead. There can be no darker or more devastating tragedy than the death of man's faith in himself and in his power to direct his future.

I salute the present generation. Hang on to one of your most precious parts of youth, laughter—don't lose it as many of you seem to have done, you need it. Together we may find some of what we're looking for—laughter, beauty, love, and the chance to create.

Saul Alinsky

RULES
FOR
RADICALS

The
Purpose

The life of man upon earth is a warfare ...

— JOB 7:1

WHAT FOLLOWS IS for those who want to change the world from what it is to what they believe it should be. *The Prince* was written by Machiavelli for the Haves on how to hold power. *Rules for Radicals* is written for the Have-Nots on how to take it away.

In this book we are concerned with how to create mass organizations to seize power and give it to the people; to realize the democratic dream of equality, justice, peace, co-operation, equal and full opportunities for education, full and useful employment, health, and the creation of those circumstances in which man can have the chance to live by values that give meaning to life. We are talking about a mass power organization which will change the world into a place where all men and women walk erect, in the spirit of that credo of the Spanish Civil War, "Better to die on your feet than to live on your knees." This means revolution.

The significant changes in history have been made by revolutions. There are people who say that it is not revolution, but evolution, that brings about change—but *evolution is simply the term used by nonparticipants to denote a particular sequence of revolutions as they synthesized into a specific major social change.* In this book I propose certain general observations, propositions, and concepts of the mechanics of mass movements and the various stages of the cycle of action and reaction in revolution. This is not an ideological book except insofar as argument for change, rather than for the status quo, can be called an ideology; different people, in different places, in different situations and different times will construct their own solutions and symbols of salvation for those times. This book will not contain any panacea or dogma; I detest and fear dogma. I know that all revolutions must have ideologies to spur them on. That in the heat of conflict these ideologies tend to be smelted into rigid dogmas claiming exclusive possession of the truth, and the keys to paradise, is tragic. Dogma is the enemy of human freedom. Dogma must be watched for and apprehended at every turn and twist of the revolutionary movement. The human spirit glows from that small inner light of doubt whether we are right, while those who believe with complete certainty that they possess the right are dark inside and darken the world outside with cruelty, pain, and injustice. Those who enshrine the poor or Have-Nots are as guilty as other dogmatists and just as dangerous. To diminish the danger that ideology will deteriorate into dogma, and to protect the free, open, questing, and creative mind of man, as well as to allow for change, no ideology should be more specific than that of America's founding fathers: "For the general welfare."

Niels Bohr, the great atomic physicist, admirably stated the civilized position on dogmatism: "Every sentence I utter must be understood not as an affirmation, but as a question." I will argue that man's hopes lie in the acceptance of the great law of change; that a general understanding of the principles of change will provide clues for rational action and an awareness of the realistic relationship between means and ends and how each determines the other. I hope that these pages will contribute to the education of the radicals of today, and to the conversion of hot, emotional, impulsive passions that are impotent and frustrating to actions that will be calculated, purposeful, and effective.

An example of the political insensitivity of many of today's so-called radicals and the lost opportunities is found in this account of an episode during the trial of the Chicago Seven:

> Over the weekend some hundred fifty lawyers, from all parts of the country, had gathered in Chicago to picket the federal building in protest against Judge Hoffman's [arrest of] the four lawyers. This delegation, which was supported by thirteen members of the faculty of Harvard Law School and which included a number of other professors as well, submitted a brief, as friend of the Court, which called Judge Hoffman's actions "a travesty of justice [which] threatens to destroy the confidence of the American people in the entire judicial process . . ." By ten o'clock the angry lawyers had begun to march around the Federal Building, where they were joined by hundreds of student radicals, several Black Panthers, and a hundred or more blue-helmeted Chicago police.
>
> Shortly before noon, about forty of the picketing lawyers carried their signs into the lobby of the Federal Building, despite the notice posted on the glass wall beside the entrance, and signed by Judge Campbell, forbidding such demonstrations within the building. Hardly had the lawyers entered, however, than Judge Campbell himself descended to the lobby, dressed in his black robes

and accompanied by a marshal, a stenographer, and his court clerk. Surrounded by the angry lawyers, who were themselves encircled by a ring of police and federal marshals, the Judge proceeded to hold Court then and there. He announced that unless the pickets withdrew immediately, he would charge them with contempt.

This time, he warned, there could be no question that their contempt would occur in the presence of the Court, and would thus be subject to summary punishment. No sooner had he made this announcement however, than a voice from the throng shouted, "Fuck you, Campbell." After a moment of tense silence, followed by a cheer from the crowd and a noticeable stiffening among the police, Judge Campbell himself withdrew. Then the lawyers, too, left the lobby and rejoined the pickets on the sidewalk.

—Jason Epstein, *The Great Conspiracy Trial*, Random House, 1970.

The picketing lawyers threw away a beautiful opportunity to create a nationwide issue. Offhand, there would seem to have been two choices, either of which would have forced the judge's hand and kept the issue going: some one of the lawyers could have stepped up to the judge after the voice said, "Fuck you, Campbell," said that the lawyers there did not support personal obscenities, but they were not leaving; or all the lawyers together could have chorused, with one voice, "Fuck you, Campbell!" They did neither; instead, they let the initiative pass from them to the judge, and achieved nothing.

Radicals must be resilient, adaptable to shifting political circumstances, and sensitive enough to the process of action and reaction to avoid being trapped by their own tactics and forced to travel a road not of their choosing. In short, radicals must have a degree of control over the flow of events.

Here I propose to present an arrangement of certain facts and general concepts of change, a step toward a science of revolution.

All societies discourage and penalize ideas and writings that threaten the ruling status quo. It is understandable, therefore, that the literature of a Have society is a veritable desert whenever we look for writings on social change. Once the American Revolution was done with, we can find very little besides the right of revolution that is laid down in the Declaration of Independence as a fundamental right; seventy-three years later Thoreau's brief essay on "The Duty of Civil Disobedience"; followed by Lincoln's reaffirmation of the revolutionary right in 1861.* There are many phrases extolling the sacredness of revolution—that is, revolutions of the past. Our enthusiasm for the sacred right of revolution is increased and enhanced with the passage of time. The older the revolution, the more it recedes into history, the more sacred it becomes. Except for Thoreau's limited remarks, our society has given us few words of advice, few suggestions of how to fertilize social change.

From the Haves, on the other hand, there has come an unceasing flood of literature justifying the status quo. Religious, economic, social, political, and legal tracts endlessly attack all revolutionary ideas and action for change as immoral, fallacious and against God, country, and mother. These literary sedations by the status quo include the threat that, since all such movements are unpatriotic,

---

* Lincoln's First Inaugural. "This country, with its institutions, belongs to the people who inhabit it. Whenever they shall grow weary of the existing government, they can exercise their constitutional right of amending it, or their revolutionary right to dismember or overthrow it."

subversive, spawned in hell and reptilian in their creeping insidiousness, dire punishments will be meted out to their supporters. All great revolutions, including Christianity, ● the various reformations, democracy, capitalism, and socialism, have suffered these epithets in the times of their birth. To the status quo concerned about its public image, revolution is the only force which has no image, but instead casts a dark, ominous shadow of things to come.

The Have-Nots of the world, swept up in their present upheavals and desperately seeking revolutionary writings, can find such literature only from the communists, both red and yellow. Here they can read about tactics, maneuvers, strategy and principles of action in the making of revolutions. Since in this literature all ideas are imbedded in the language of communism, revolution appears synonymous with communism.● When, in the throes of their revolutionary fervor, the Have-Nots hungrily turn to us in their first steps from starvation to subsistence, we respond with a bewildering, unbelievable, and meaningless conglomeration of abstractions about freedom, morality, equality, and the danger of intellectual enslavement by communistic ideology! This is accompanied by charitable handouts dressed up in ribbons of moral principle and

---

● U. S. Supreme Court Justice William O. Douglas, "The U. S. and Revolution," Center for the Study of Democratic Institutions Occasional Paper No. 116: "On trips to Asia I often asked men in their thirties and forties what they were reading when they were eighteen. They usually answered 'Karl Marx'; and when I asked them why, they replied, 'We were under colonial rule, seeking a way out. We wanted our independence. To get it we had to make revolution. The only books on revolution were published by the communists.' These men almost invariably had repudiated communism as a political cult, retaining, however, a tinge of socialism. As I talked with them, I came to realize the great opportunities we missed when we became preoccupied in fighting communism with bombs and with dollars, rather than with ideas of revolution, of freedom, of justice."

"freedom," with the price tag of unqualified political loyalty to us. With the coming of the Revolutions in Russia and China we suddenly underwent a moral conversion and became concerned for the welfare of our brothers all over the world. *Revolution by the Have-Nots has a way of inducing a moral revelation among the Haves.*

Revolution by the Have-Nots also induces a paranoid fear; now, therefore, we find every corrupt and repressive government the world around saying to us, "Give us money and soldiers or there will be a revolution and the new leaders will be your enemies." Fearful of revolution and identifying ourselves as the status quo, we have permitted the communists to assume by default the revolutionary halo of justice for the Have-Nots. We then compound this mistake by assuming that the status quo everywhere must be defended and buttressed against revolution. Today revolution has become synonymous with communism while capitalism is synonymous with status quo. Occasionally we will accept a revolution if it is guaranteed to be on our side, and then only when we realize that the revolution is inevitable. We abhor revolutions.

We have permitted a suicidal situation to unfold wherein revolution and communism have become one. These pages are committed to splitting this political atom, separating this exclusive identification of communism with revolution. If it were possible for the Have-Nots of the world to recognize and accept the idea that revolution did not inevitably mean hate and war, cold or hot, from the United States, that alone would be a great revolution in world politics and the future of man. This is a major reason for my attempt to provide a revolutionary handbook not cast in a communist *or* capitalist mold, but as a manual for the Have-Nots of the world regardless of the color of their skins or their politics. My aim here is to suggest how to organize for power: how to get it and to use it. I will argue that the failure to use power for a more equitable distribution of the means of life for all people signals the end of the revolution and the start of the counterrevolution.

Revolution has always advanced with an ideological spear just as the status quo has inscribed its ideology upon its shield. All of life is partisan. There is no dispassionate objectivity. The revolutionary ideology is not confined to a specific limited formula. It is a series of general principles, rooted in Lincoln's May 19, 1856, statement: "Be not deceived. Revolutions do not go backward."

THE IDEOLOGY OF CHANGE

This raises the question: what, if any, is my ideology? What kind of ideology, if any, can an organizer have who is working in and for a free society? The prerequisite for an ideology is possession of a basic truth. For example, a Marxist begins with his prime truth that all evils are caused by the exploitation of the proletariat by the capitalists. From this he logically proceeds to the revolution to end capitalism, then into the third stage of reorganization into a new social order or the dictatorship of the proletariat, and finally the last stage—the political paradise of communism. The Christians also begin with their prime truth: the divinity of Christ and the tripartite nature of God. Out of these "prime truths" flow a step-by-step ideology.

An organizer working in and for an open society is in an ideological dilemma. To begin with, he does not have a fixed truth—truth to him is relative and changing; *everything* to him is relative and changing. He is a politcal relativist. He accepts the late Justice Learned Hand's statement that "the mark of a free man is that ever-gnawing inner uncertainty as to whether or not he is right." The consequence is that he is ever on the hunt for the causes of man's plight and the general propositions that help to make some sense out of man's irrational world. He must constantly examine life, including his own, to get some idea of what it is all about, and he must challenge and test his own findings. Irreverence, essential to questioning, is a requisite. Curiosity becomes compulsive. His most frequent word is "why?"*

Does this then mean that the organizer in a free society for a free society is rudderless? No, I believe that he has a far better sense of direction and compass than the closed-society organizer with his rigid political ideology. First, the free-society organizer is loose, resilient, fluid, and on the move in a society which is itself in a state of constant change. To the extent that he is free from the shackles of dogma, he can respond to the realities of the widely different situations our society presents. In the end he has one conviction—a belief that if people have the power to act, in the long run they will, most of the time, reach the right decisions. The alternative to this would be rule by the elite—either a dictatorship or some form of a political aristocracy. I am not concerned if this faith in people is regarded as a prime truth and therefore a contradiction of what I have already written, for life is a story of contradictions. Believing in people, the radical has the job of organizing them so that they will have the power and opportunity to best

---

* Some say it's no coincidence that the question mark is an inverted plow, breaking up the hard soil of old beliefs and preparing for the new growth.

meet each unforeseeable future crisis as they move ahead in their eternal search for those values of equality, justice, freedom, peace, a deep concern for the preciousness of human life, and all those rights and values propounded by Judaeo-Christianity and the democratic political tradition. Democracy is not an end but the best means toward achieving these values. This is my credo for which I live and, if need be, die.

The basic requirement for the understanding of the politics of change is to recognize the world as it is. We must work with it on its terms if we are to change it to the kind of world we would like it to be. We must first see the world as it is and not as we would like it to be. We must see the world as all political realists have, in terms of "what men do and not what they ought to do," as Machiavelli and others have put it.

It is painful to accept fully the simple fact that one begins from where one is, that one must break free of the web of illusions one spins about life. Most of us view the world not as it is but as we would like it to be. The preferred world can be seen any evening on television in the succession of programs where the good always wins —that is, until the late evening newscast, when suddenly we are plunged into the world as it is.*

Political realists see the world as it is: an arena of power politics moved primarily by perceived immediate self-interests, where morality is rhetorical rationale for expe-

---

* With some exceptions. In one of America's Shangri-Las of escape from the world as it is, Carmel-by-the-Sea, California, on the coast of the beautiful Monterey Peninsula, radio station KRML used to broadcast the "Sunshine News—which headlines the positive, only the good news of the world!"

Intellectuals, who would scoff at "Sunshine News," are no exception to the preference for already-formulated answers.

dient action and self-interest. Two examples would be the priest who wants to be a bishop and bootlicks and politicks his way up, justifying it with the rationale, "After I get to be bishop I'll use my office for Christian reformation," or the businessman who reasons, "First I'll make my million and after that I'll go for the real things in life." Unfortunately one changes in many ways on the road to the bishopric or the first million, and then one says, "I'll wait until I'm a cardinal and then I can be more effective," or, "I can do a lot more after I get two million"—and so it goes.* In this world laws are written for the lofty aim of "the common good" and then acted out in life on the basis of the common greed. In this world irrationality clings to man like his shadow so that the right things are done for the wrong reasons—afterwards, we dredge up the right reasons for justification. It is a world not of angels but of angles, where men speak of moral principles but act on power principles; a world where we are always moral and our enemies always immoral; a world where "reconciliation" means that when one side gets the power and the other side gets reconciled to it, then we have reconciliation; a world of religious institutions that have, in the main, come to support and justify the status quo

---

* Each year, for a number of years, the activists in the graduating class from a major Catholic seminary near Chicago would visit me for a day just before their ordination, with questions about values, revolutionary tactics, and such. Once, at the end of such a day, one of the seminarians said, "Mr. Alinsky, before we came here we met and agreed that there was one question we particularly wanted to put to you. We're going to be ordained, and then we'll be assigned to different parishes, as assistants to—frankly—stuffy, reactionary, old pastors. They will disapprove of a lot of what you and we believe in, and we will be put into a killing routine. Our question is: how do we keep our faith in true Christian values, everything we hope to do to change the system?"

That was easy. I answered, "When you go out that door, just make your own personal decision about whether you want to be a bishop or a priest, and everything else will follow."

so that today organized religion is materially solvent and spiritually bankrupt. We live with a Judaeo-Christian ethic that has not only accommodated itself to but justified slavery, war, and every other ugly human exploitation of whichever status quo happened to prevail:

We live in a world where "good" is a value dependent on whether we want it. In the world as it is, the solution of each problem inevitably creates a new one. In the world as it is there are no permanent happy or sad endings. Such endings belong to the world of fantasy, the world as we would like it to be, the world of children's fairy tales where "they lived happily ever after." In the world as it is, the stream of events surges endlessly onward with death as the only terminus. One never reaches the horizon; it is always just beyond, ever beckoning onward; it is the pursuit of life itself. This is the world as it is. This is where you start.

It is not a world of peace and beauty and dispassionate rationality, but as Henry James once wrote, "Life *is*, in fact, a battle. Evil is insolent and strong; beauty enchanting but rare; goodness very apt to be weak; folly very apt to be defiant; wickedness to carry the day; imbeciles to be in great places, people of sense in small, and mankind generally unhappy. But the world as it stands is no narrow illusion, no phantasm, no evil dream of the night; we wake up to it again forever and ever; and we can neither forget it nor deny it nor dispense with it." Henry James's statement is an affirmation of that of Job: "The life of man upon earth is a warfare . . ." Disraeli put it succinctly: "Political life must be taken as you find it."

Once we have moved into the world as it is then we begin to shed fallacy after fallacy. The prime illusion we must rid ourselves of is the conventional view in which things are seen separate from their inevitable counterparts.

We know intellectually that everthing is functionally inter-related, but in our operations we segment and isolate all values and issues. Everything about us must be seen as the indivisible partner of its converse, light and darkness, good and evil, life and death. From the moment we are born we begin to die. Happiness and misery are inseparable. So are peace and war. The threat of destruction from nuclear energy conversely carries the opportunity of peace and plenty, and so with every component of this universe; all is paired in this enormous Noah's Ark of life.

Life seems to lack rhyme or reason or even a shadow of order unless we approach it with the key of converses. Seeing everything in its duality, we begin to get some dim clues to direction and what it's all about. It is in these contradictions and their incessant interacting tensions that creativity begins. As we begin to accept the concept of contradictions we see every problem or issue in its whole, inter-related sense. We then recognize that for every positive there is a negative,* and that there is nothing positive with-out its concomitant negative, nor any political paradise without its negative side.

Niels Bohr pointed out that the appearance of contradictions was a signal that the experiment was on the right track: "There is not much hope if we have only one difficulty, but when we have two, we can match them off against each other." Bohr called this "complementarity,"

---

* For more than four thousand years the Chinese have been familiar with the principle of complementarity in their philosophical life. They believe that from the illimitable (nature, God or gods) came the principle of creation which they called the Great Extreme and from the Great Extreme came the Two Principles or Dual Powers, Yang and Yin, out of which came everything else. Yang and Yin have been defined as positive and negative, light and darkness, male and female, or numerous other examples of opposites or converses.

meaning that the interplay of seemingly conflicting forces or opposites is the actual harmony of nature. Whitehead similarly observed, "In formal logic, a contradiction is the signal of a defeat; but in the evolution of real knowledge it marks the first step in progress towards a victory."

Everywhere you look all change shows this complementarity. In Chicago the people of Upton Sinclair's *Jungle,* then the worst slum in America, crushed by starvation wages when they worked, demoralized, diseased, living in rotting shacks, were organized. Their banners proclaimed equality for all races, job security, and a decent life for all. With their power they fought and won. Today, as part of the middle class, they are also part of our racist, discriminatory culture.

The Tennessee Valley Authority was one of the prize jewels in the democratic crown. Visitors came from every part of the world to see, admire, and study this physical and social achievement of a free society. Today it is the scourge of the Cumberland Mountains, strip mining for coal and wreaking havoc on the countryside.

The C.I.O. was the militant champion of America's workers. In its ranks, directly and indirectly, were all of America's radicals; they fought the corporate structure of the nation and won. Today, merged with the A.F. of L., it is an entrenched member of the establishment and its leader supports the war in Vietnam.

Another example is today's high-rise public housing projects. Originally conceived and carried through as major advances in ridding cities of slums, they involved the tearing down of rotting, rat-infested tenements, and the erection of modern apartment buildings. They were acclaimed as America's refusal to permit its people to live in the dirty shambles of the slums. It is common knowledge that they have turned into jungles of horror and now confront us with the problem of how we can either convert or get rid of

them. They have become compounds of double segregation
—on the bases of both economy and race—and a danger for
anyone compelled to live in these projects. A beautiful
positive dream has grown into a negative nightmare.

It is the universal tale of revolution and reaction. It is
the constant struggle between the positive and its converse
negative, which includes the reversal of roles so that the
positive of today is the negative of tomorrow and vice versa.

This view of nature recognizes that reality is dual. The
principles of quantum mechanics in physics apply even
more dramatically to the mechanics of mass movements.
This is true not only in "complementarity" but in the repudiation of the hitherto universal concept of causality, whereby
matter and physics were understood in terms of cause
and effect, where for every effect there had to be a cause and
one always produced the other. In quantum mechanics,
causality was largely replaced by probability: an electron or
atom did not have to do anything specific in response to a
particular force; there was just a set of probabilities that it
would react in this or that way. This is fundamental in the
observations and propositions which follow. At no time in
any discussion or analysis of mass movements, tactics, or any
other phase of the problem, can it be said that if this is done
then that will result. The most we can hope to achieve is an
understanding of the probabilities consequent to certain
actions.

This grasp of the duality of all phenomena is vital in
our understanding of politics. It frees one from the myth
that one approach is positive and another negative. There
is no such thing in life. One man's positive is another
man's negative. The description of any procedure as "positive" or "negative" is the mark of a political illiterate.

Once the nature of revolution is understood from the
dualistic outlook we lose our mono-view of a revolution and

see it coupled with its inevitable counterrevolution. Once we accept and learn to anticipate the inevitable counter-revolution, we may then alter the historical pattern of revolution and counterrevolution from the traditional slow advance of two steps forward and one step backward to minimizing the latter. Each element with its positive and converse sides is fused to other related elements in an end-less series of everything, so that the converse of revolution on one side is counterrevolution and on the other side, refor-mation, and so on in an endless chain of connected con-verses.

CLASS DISTINCTIONS: THE TRINITY

The setting for the drama of change has never varied. Man-kind has been and is divided into three parts: the Haves, the Have-Nots, and the Have-a-Little, Want Mores.

On top are the Haves with power, money, food, se-curity, and luxury. They suffocate in their surpluses while the Have-Nots starve. Numerically the Haves have always been the fewest. The Haves want to keep things as they are and are opposed to change. Thermopolitically they are cold and determined to freeze the status quo.

On the bottom are the world's Have-Nots. On the world scene they are by far the greatest in numbers. They are chained together by the common misery of poverty, rotten housing, disease, ignorance, political impotence, and despair; when they are employed their jobs pay the least and they are deprived in all areas basic to human growth. Caged by color, physical or political, they are barred from an opportunity to represent themselves in the politics of life. The Haves want to keep; the Have-Nots want to get. Thermopolitically they are a mass of cold ashes of resignation and fatalism, but inside there are glowing embers of hope which can be fanned by the building of means of obtaining power. Once the fever begins the flame will follow. They have nowhere to go but up.

They hate the establishment of the Haves with its arrogant opulence, its police, its courts, and its churches. Justice, morality, law, and order, are mere words when used by the Haves, which justify and secure their status quo. The power of the Have-Nots rests only with their numbers. It has been said that the Haves, living under the nightmare of possible threats to their possessions, are always faced with the question of "when do we sleep?" while the perennial question of the Have-Nots is "when do we eat?" The cry of the Have-Nots has never been "give us your hearts" but always "get off our backs"; they ask not for love but for breathing space.

Between the Haves and Have-Nots are the Have-a-Little, Want Mores—the middle class. Torn between upholding the status quo to protect the little they have, yet wanting change so they can get more, they become split personalities. They could be described as social, economic, and political schizoids. Generally, they seek the safe way, where they can profit by change and yet not risk losing the little they have. They insist on a minimum of three aces before playing a hand in the poker game of revolution. Thermopolitically they are tepid and rooted in inertia. Today in Western society and particularly in the United States they comprise the majority of our population.

Yet in the conflicting interests and contradictions within the Have-a-Little, Want Mores is the genesis of creativity. Out of this class have come, with few exceptions, the great world leaders of change of the past centuries:

Moses, Paul of Tarsus, Martin Luther, Robespierre, Georges Danton, Samuel Adams, Alexander Hamilton, Thomas Jefferson, Napoleon Bonaparte, Giuseppe Garibaldi, Nikolai Lenin, Mahatma Gandhi, Fidel Castro, Mao Tse-tung, and others.

Just as the clash of interests within the Have-a-Little, Want Mores has bred so many of the great leaders it has also spawned a particular breed stalemated by cross interests into inaction. These Do-Nothings profess a commitment to social change for ideals of justice, equality, and opportunity, and then abstain from and discourage all effective action for change. They are known by their brand, "I agree with your ends but not your means." They function as blankets whenever possible smothering sparks of dissension that promise to flare up into the fire of action. These Do-Nothings appear publicly as good men, humanitarian, concerned with justice and dignity. In practice they are invidious. They are the ones Edmund Burke referred to when he said, acidly: "The only thing necessary for the triumph of evil is for good men to do nothing." Both the revolutionary leaders, or the Doers, and the Do-Nothings will be examined in these pages.

The history of prevailing status quos shows decay and decadence infecting the opulent materialism of the Haves. The spiritual life of the Haves is a ritualistic justification of their possessions.

More than one hundred years ago, Tocqueville commented, as did other students of America at that time, that self-indulgence accompanied by concern for nothing except personal materialistic welfare was the major menace to America's future. Whitehead noted in *Adventures of Ideas* that "The enjoyment of power is fatal to the subtleties of life. Ruling classes degenerate by reason of their lazy indulgence in obvious gratifications." In such a state men may be said to fall asleep, for it is in sleep that we each turn away from the world about us to our private worlds.* I must quote one more book pertinent to this subject: in *Alice in Wonderland*, Tiger-Lily explains about the talking flowers to Alice. Tiger-Lily points out that the flowers that talk grow out of hard beds of ground and "in most gardens," Tiger-Lily says, "they make the beds too soft—so that the flowers are always asleep." It is as though the great law of change had prepared the anesthesization of the victim prior to the social surgery to come.

Change means movement. Movement means friction. Only in the frictionless vacuum of a nonexistent abstract world can movement or change occur without that abrasive friction of conflict. In these pages it is our open political purpose to cooperate with the great law of change; to want otherwise would be like King Canute's commanding the tides and waves to cease.

A word about my personal philosophy. It is anchored in optimism. It must be, for optimism brings with it hope, a future with a purpose, and therefore, a will to fight for a better world. Without this optimism, there is no reason to carry on. If we think of the struggle as a climb up a mountain, then we must visualize a mountain with no top. We see a top, but when we finally reach it, the overcast rises and we find ourselves merely on a bluff. The mountain continues on up. Now we see the "real" top ahead of us, and strive for it, only to find we've reached another bluff, the top still above us. And so it goes on, interminably.

Knowing that the mountain has no top, that it is a perpetual quest from plateau to plateau, the question arises, "Why the struggle, the conflict, the heartbreak, the danger, the sacrifice. Why the constant climb?" Our answer is the

---

* Heraclitus, *Fragments*: "The waking have one world in common; sleepers have each a private world of his own."

same as that which a real mountain climber gives when he is asked why he does what he does. "Because it's there." Because life is there ahead of you and either one tests oneself in its challenges or huddles in the valleys in a dreamless day-to-day existence whose only purpose is the preservation of an illusory security and safety. The latter is what the vast majority of people choose to do, fearing the adventure into the unknown. Paradoxically, they give up the dream of what may lie ahead on the heights of tomorrow for a perpetual nightmare—an endless succession of days fearing the loss of a tenuous security.

Unlike the chore of the mythic Sisyphis, this challenge is not an endless pushing up of a boulder to the top of a hill, only to have it roll back again, the chore to be repeated eternally. It is pushing the boulder up an endless mountain, but, unlike Sisyphis, we are always going further upward. And also unlike Sisyphis, each stage of the trail upward is different, newly dramatic, an adventure each time.

At times we do fall back and become discouraged, but it is not that we are making no progress. Simply, this is the very nature of life—that it is a climb—and that the resolution of each issue in turn creates other issues, born of plights which are unimaginable today. The pursuit of happiness is never-ending; happiness lies in the pursuit.

Confronted with the materialistic decadence of the status quo, one should not be surprised to find that all revolutionary movements are primarily generated from spiritual values and considerations of justice, equality, peace, and brotherhood. History is a relay of revolutions; the torch of idealism is carried by the revolutionary group until this group becomes an establishment, and then quietly the torch is put down to wait until a new revolutionary group picks it up for the next leg of the run. Thus the revolutionary cycle goes on.

A major revolution to be won in the immediate future is the dissipation of man's illusion that his own welfare can be separate from that of all others. As long as man is shackled to this myth, so long will the human spirit languish. Concern for our private, material well-being with disregard for the well-being of others is immoral according to the precepts of our Judaeo-Christian civilization, but worse, it is stupidity worthy of the lower animals. It is man's foot still dragging in the primeval slime of his beginnings, in ignorance and mere animal cunning. But those who know the interdependence of man to be his major strength in the struggle out of the muck have not been wise in their exhortations and moral pronouncements that man is his brother's keeper. On that score the record of the past centuries has been a disaster, for it was wrong to assume that man would pursue morality on a level higher than his day-to-day living demanded; it was a disservice to the future to separate morality from man's daily desires and elevate it to a plane of altruism and self-sacrifice. The fact is that it is not man's "better nature" but his self-interest that demands that he be his brother's keeper. We now live in a world where no man can have a loaf of bread while his neighbor has none. If he does not share his bread, he dare not sleep, for his neighbor will kill him. To eat and sleep in safety man must do the right thing, if for seemingly the wrong reasons, and be in practice his brother's keeper

I believe that man is about to learn that the most practical life is the moral life and that the moral life is the only road to survival. He is beginning to learn that he will either share part of his material wealth or lose all of it; that he will respect and learn to live with other political ideologies if he wants civilization to go on. This is the kind of argument that man's actual experience equips him to understand and accept. *This is the low road to morality. There is no other.*

Of Means
and Ends

We cannot think first and act afterwards. From the moment of birth we are immersed in action and can only fitfully guide it by taking thought.

— ALFRED NORTH WHITEHEAD

THAT PERENNIAL QUESTION, "Does the end justify the means?" is meaningless as it stands; the real and only question regarding the ethics of means and ends is, and always has been, "Does this *particular* end justify this *particular* means?"

Life and how you live it is the story of means and ends. The *end* is what you want, and the *means* is how you get it. Whenever we think about social change, the question of means and ends arises. The man of action views the issue of means and ends in pragmatic and strategic terms. He has no other problem; he thinks only of his actual resources and the possibilities of various choices of action. He asks of ends only whether they are achievable and worth the cost; of means, only whether they will work. To say that corrupt means corrupt the ends is to believe in the immaculate conception of ends and principles. The real arena is corrupt and bloody. Life is a corrupting process from the time a child learns to play his mother off against his father in the politics of when to go to bed; he who fears corruption fears life.

The practical revolutionary will understand Goethe's "conscience is the virtue of observers and not of agents of action"; in action, one does not always enjoy the luxury of a decision that is consistent both with one's individual conscience and the good of mankind. The choice must always be for the latter. Action is for mass salvation and not for the individual's personal salvation. He who sacrifices the mass good for his personal conscience has a peculiar conception of "personal salvation"; he doesn't care enough for people to be "corrupted" for them.

The men who pile up the heaps of discussion and literature on the ethics of means and ends—which with rare exception is conspicuous for its sterility—rarely write about their own experiences in the perpetual struggle of life and change. They are strangers, moreover, to the burdens and problems of operational responsibility and the unceasing pressure for immediate decisions. They are passionately committed to a mystical objectivity where passions are suspect. They assume a nonexistent situation where men dispassionately and with reason draw and devise means and ends as if studying a navigational chart on land. They can be recognized by one of two verbal brands: "We agree with the ends but not the means," or "This is not the time." *The means-and-end moralists or non-doers always wind up on their ends without any means.*

The means-and-ends moralists, constantly obsessed with the ethics of the means used by the Have-Nots against the Haves, should search themselves as to their real political position. In fact, they are passive—but real—allies of the Haves. They are the ones Jacques Maritain referred to in his statement, "The fear of soiling ourselves by entering the context of history is not virtue, but a way of escaping virtue." These non-doers were the ones who chose not to fight the Nazis in the only way they could have been fought; they were the ones who drew their window blinds to shut out the shameful spectacle of Jews and political prisoners being dragged through the streets; they were the ones who privately deplored the horror of it all—and did nothing. This is the nadir of immorality. The most unethical of all means is the non-use of any means. It is this species of man who so vehemently and militantly participated in that classically idealistic debate at the old League of Nations on the ethical differences between defensive and offensive weapons. Their fears of action drive them to refuge in an ethics so divorced from the politics of life that it can apply only to angels, not to men. The standards of judgment must be rooted in the whys and wherefores of life as it is lived, the world as it is, not our wished-for fantasy of the world as it should be.

I present here a series of rules pertaining to the ethics of means and ends: first, that *one's concern with the ethics of means and ends varies inversely with one's personal interest in the issue.* When we are not directly concerned our morality overflows; as La Rochefoucauld put it, "We all have strength enough to endure the misfortunes of others." Accompanying this rule is the parallel one that *one's concern with the ethics of means and ends varies inversely with one's distance from the scene of conflict.*

The second rule of the ethics of means and ends is that the judgment of the ethics of means is dependent upon the political position of those sitting in judgment. If you actively opposed the Nazi occupation and joined the underground Resistance, then you adopted the means of assassination, terror, property destruction, the bombing of tunnels and trains, kidnapping, and the willingness to sacrifice innocent hostages to the end of defeating the Nazis. Those who opposed the Nazi conquerors regarded the Resistance as a secret army of selfless, patriotic idealists, courageous beyond expectation and willing to sacrifice their lives to their moral convictions. To the occupation authorities, however, these people were lawless terrorists, murderers, saboteurs, assassins, who believed that the end justified the means, and were utterly unethical according to the mystical rules of war. Any foreign occupation would so ethically judge its opposition. However, in such conflict, neither protagonist is concerned with any value except victory. It is life or death.

To us the Declaration of Independence is a glorious document and an affirmation of human rights. To the British, on the other hand, it was a statement notorious for its deceit by omission. In the Declaration of Independence, the Bill of Particulars attesting to the reasons for the Revolution cited all of the injustices which the colonists felt that England had been guilty of, but listed none of the benefits. There was no mention of the food the colonies had received from the British Empire during times of famine, medicine during times of disease, soldiers during times of war with the Indians and other foes, or the many other direct and indirect aids to the survival of the colonies. Neither was there notice of the growing number of allies and friends of the colonists in the British House of Commons, and the hope for imminent remedial legislation to correct the inequities under which the colonies suffered.

Jefferson, Franklin, and others were honorable men, but they knew that the Declaration of Independence was

a call to war. They also knew that a list of many of the
constructive benefits of the British Empire to the colonists
would have so diluted the urgency of the call to arms for
the Revolution as to have been self-defeating. The result
might well have been a document attesting to the fact
that justice weighted down the scale at least 60 per cent
on our side, and only 40 per cent on their side; and that
because of that 20 per cent difference we were going to
have a Revolution. To expect a man to leave his wife, his
children, and his home, to leave his crops standing in the
field and pick up a gun and join the Revolutionary Army
for a 20 per cent difference in the balance of human justice
was to defy common sense.

The Declaration of Independence, as a declaration
of war, had to be what it was, a 100 per cent statement
of the justice of the cause of the colonists and a 100 per
cent denunciation of the role of the British government
as evil and unjust. Our cause had to be all shining
justice, allied with the angels; theirs had to be all evil,
tied to the Devil; in no war has the enemy or the cause
ever been gray. Therefore, from one point of view the
omission was justified; from the other, it was deliberate
deceit.

History is made up of "moral" judgments based on
politics. We condemned Lenin's acceptance of money
from the Germans in 1917 but were discreetly silent while
our Colonel William B. Thompson in the same year con-
tributed a million dollars to the anti-Bolsheviks in Russia.
As allies of the Soviets in World War II we praised and
cheered communist guerrilla tactics when the Russians
used them against the Nazis during the Nazi invasion of
the Soviet Union; we denounce the same tactics when
they are used by communist forces in different parts of

the world against us. The opposition's means, used against us, are always immoral and our means are always ethical and rooted in the highest of human values. George Bernard Shaw, in *Man and Superman,* pointed out the variations in ethical definitions by virtue of where you stand. Mendoza said to Tanner, "I am a brigand; I live by robbing the rich." Tanner replied, "I am a gentleman; I live by robbing the poor. Shake hands."

The third rule of the ethics of means and ends is that in war the end justifies almost any means. Agreements on the Geneva rules on treatment of prisoners or use of nuclear weapons are observed only because the enemy or his potential allies may retaliate.

Winston Churchill's remarks to his private secretary a few hours before the Nazis invaded the Soviet Union graphically pointed out the politics of means and ends in war. Informed of the imminent turn of events, the secretary inquired how Churchill, the leading British anti-communist, could reconcile himself to being on the same side as the Soviets. Would not Churchill find it embarrassing and difficult to ask his government to support the communists? Churchill's reply was clear and unequivocal: "Not at all. I have only one purpose, the destruction of Hitler, and my life is much simplified thereby. If Hitler invaded Hell I would make at least a favorable reference to the Devil in the House of Commons."

In the Civil War President Lincoln did not hesitate to suspend the right of habeas corpus and to ignore the directive of the Chief Justice of the United States. Again, when Lincoln was convinced that the use of military commissions to try civilians was necessary, he brushed aside the illegality of this action with the statement that it was "indispensable to the public safety." He believed that the civil courts were powerless to cope with the in-surrectionist activities of civilians. "Must I shoot a simple-minded soldier boy who deserts, while I must not touch a hair of a wily agitator who induces him to desert . . ."

The fourth rule of the ethics of means and ends is that judgment must be made in the context of the times in which the action occurred and not from any other chronological vantage point. The Boston Massacre is a case in point. "British atrocities alone, however, were not sufficient to convince the people that murder had been done on the night of March 5: There was a deathbed confession of Patrick Carr, that the townspeople had been the aggressors and that the soldiers had fired in self defense. This unlooked-for recantation from one of the martyrs who was dying in the odor of sanctity with which Sam Adams had vested them sent a wave of alarm through the patriot ranks. But Adams blasted Carr's testimony in the eyes of all pious New Englanders by pointing out that he was an Irish 'papist' who had probably died in the confession of the Roman Catholic Church. After Sam Adams had finished with Patrick Carr even Tories did not dare to quote him to prove Bostonians were responsible for the Massacre."* To the British this was a false, rotten use of bigotry and an immoral means characteristic of the Revolutionaries, or the Sons of Liberty. To the Sons of Liberty and to the patriots, Sam Adams' action was bril-liant strategy and a God-sent lifesaver. Today we may look back and regard Adams' action in the same light as the British did, but remember that we are not today in-volved in a revolution against the British Empire.

Ethical standards must be elastic to stretch with

---

* *Sam Adams, Pioneer in Propaganda,* by John C. Miller.

the times. In politics, the ethics of means and ends can be understood by the rules suggested here. History is made up of little else but examples such as our position on freedom of the high seas in 1812 and 1917 contrasted with our 1962 blockade of Cuba, or our alliance in 1942 with the Soviet Union against Germany, Japan and Italy, and the reversal in alignments in less than a decade.

Lincoln's suspension of habeas corpus, his defiance of a directive of the Chief Justice of the United States, and the illegal use of military commissions to try civilians, were by the same man who had said in Springfield, fifteen years earlier: "Let me not be understood as saying that there are no bad laws, or that grievances may not arise for the redress of which no legal provisions have been made. I mean to say no such thing. But I do mean to say that although bad laws, if they exist, should be repealed, still, while they continue in force, for the sake of example, they should be religiously observed."

This was also the same Lincoln who, a few years prior to his signing the Emancipation Proclamation, stated in his First Inaugural Address: "I do but quote from one of those speeches when I declared that 'I have no purpose, directly or indirectly, to interfere with the institution of slavery in the States where it exists. I believe I have no lawful right to do so, and I have no inclination to do so.' Those who nominated and elected me did so with full knowledge that I made this and many similar declarations and have never recanted them."

Those who would be critical of the ethics of Lincoln's reversal of positions have a strangely unreal picture of a static unchanging world, where one remains firm and committed to certain so-called principles or positions. In the politics of human life, consistency is not a virtue. To be consistent means, according to the Oxford Universal Dictionary, "standing still or not moving." Men must change with the times or die.

The change in Jefferson's orientation when he became President is pertinent to this point. Jefferson had incessantly attacked President Washington for using national self-interest as the point of departure for all decisions. He castigated the President as narrow and selfish and argued that decisions should be made on a world-interest basis to encourage the spread of the ideas of the American Revolution; that Washington's adherence to the criteria of national self-interest was a betrayal of the American Revolution. However, from the first moment when Jefferson assumed the presidency of the United States his every decision was dictated by national self-interest. This story from another century has parallels in our century and every other.

The fifth rule of the ethics of means and ends is that concern with ethics increases with the number of means available and vice versa. To the man of action the first criterion in determining which means to employ is to assess what means are available. Reviewing and selecting available means is done on a straight utilitarian basis— will it work? Moral questions may enter when one chooses among equally effective alternate means. But if one lacks the luxury of a choice and is possessed of only one means, then the ethical question will never arise; automatically the lone means becomes endowed with a moral spirit. Its defense lies in the cry, "What else could I do?" Inversely, the secure position in which one possesses the choice of a number of effective and powerful means is always accompanied by that ethical concern and serenity of conscience so admirably described by Mark Twain as "The calm confidence of a Christian holding four aces."

To me ethics is doing what is best for the most. During a conflict with a major corporation I was confronted with a threat of public exposure of a photograph of a motel "Mr. & Mrs." registration and photographs of my girl and myself. I said, "Go ahead and give it to the press. I think she's beautiful and I have never claimed to be celibate. Go ahead!" That ended the threat.

Almost on the heels of this encounter one of the corporation's minor executives came to see me. It turned out that he was a secret sympathizer with our side. Pointing to his briefcase, he said: "In there is plenty of proof that so and so [a leader of the opposition] prefers boys to girls." I said, "Thanks, but forget it. I don't fight that way. I don't want to see it. Goodbye." He protested, "But they just tried to hang you on that girl." I replied, "The fact that they fight that way doesn't mean I have to do it. To me, dragging a person's private life into this muck is loathsome and nauseous." He left.

So far, so noble; *but,* if I had been convinced that the only way we could win was to use it, then without any reservations I would have used it. What was my alternative? To draw myself up into righteous "moral" indignation saying, "I would rather lose than corrupt my principles," and then go home with my ethical hymen intact? The fact that 40,000 poor would lose their war against hopelessness and despair was just too tragic. That their condition would even be worsened by the vindictiveness of the corporation was also terrible and unfortunate, but that's life. After all, one has to remember means and ends. It's true that I might have trouble getting to sleep because it takes time to tuck those big, angelic, moral wings under the covers. To me that would be utter immorality.

The sixth rule of the ethics of means and ends is that the less important the end to be desired, the more one can afford to engage in ethical evaluations of means.

The seventh rule of the ethics of means and ends is that generally success or failure is a mighty determinant of ethics. The judgment of history leans heavily on the outcome of success or failure; it spells the difference between the traitor and the patriotic hero. *There can be no such thing as a successful traitor, for if one succeeds he becomes a founding father.*

The eighth rule of the ethics of means and ends is that the morality of a means depends upon whether the means is being employed at a time of imminent defeat or imminent victory. The same means employed with victory seemingly assured may be defined as immoral, whereas if it had been used in desperate circumstances to avert defeat, the question of morality would never arise. In short, ethics are determined by whether one is losing or winning. From the beginning of time killing has always been regarded as justifiable if committed in self-defense.

Let us confront this principle with the most awful ethical question of modern times: did the United States have the right to use the atomic bomb at Hiroshima?

When we dropped the atomic bomb the United States was assured of victory. In the Pacific, Japan had suffered an unbroken succession of defeats. Now we were in Okinawa with an air base from which we could bomb the enemy around the clock. The Japanese air force was decimated, as was their navy. Victory had come in Europe, and the entire European air force, navy, and army were released for use in the Pacific. Russia was moving in for a cut of the spoils. Defeat for Japan was an absolute certainty and the only question was how and when the coup de grâce would be administered. For familiar reasons we dropped the bomb and triggered off as well a universal debate on the morality of the use of this means for the end of finishing the war.

I submit that if the atomic bomb had been developed shortly after Pearl Harbor when we stood defenseless; when most of our Pacific fleet was at the bottom of the sea; when the nation was fearful of invasion on the Pacific coast; when we were committed as well to the war in Europe, that then the use of the bomb at that time on Japan would have been universally heralded as a just retribution of hail, fire, and brimstone. Then the use of the bomb would have been hailed as proof that good inevitably triumphs over evil. The question of the ethics of the use of the bomb would never have arisen at that time and the character of the present debate would have been very different. Those who would disagree with this assertion have no memory of the state of the world at that time. They are either fools or liars or both.

The ninth rule of the ethics of means and ends is that any effective means is automatically judged by the opposition as being unethical. One of our greatest revolutionary heroes was Francis Marion of South Carolina, who became immortalized in American history as "the Swamp Fox." Marion was an outright revolutionary guerrilla. He and his men operated according to the traditions and with all of the tactics commonly associated with the present-day guerrillas. Cornwallis and the regular British Army found their plans and operations harried and disorganized by Marion's guerrilla tactics. Infuriated by the effectiveness of his operations, and incapable of coping with them, the

British denounced him as a criminal and charged that he did not engage in warfare "like a gentleman" or "a Christian." He was subjected to an unremitting denunciation about his lack of ethics and morality for his use of guerrilla means to the end of winning the Revolution.

The tenth rule of the ethics of means and ends is that you do what you can with what you have and clothe it with moral garments. In the field of action, the first question that arises in the determination of means to be employed for particular ends is what means are available. This requires an assessment of whatever strengths or resources are present and can be used. It involves sifting the multiple factors which combine in creating the circumstances at any given time, and an adjustment to the popular views and the popular climate. Questions such as how much time is necessary or available must be considered. Who, and how many, will support the action? Does the opposition possess the power to the degree that it can suspend or change the laws? Does its control of police power extend to the point where legal and orderly change is impossible? If weapons are needed, then are appropriate weapons available? Availability of means determines whether you will be underground or above ground; whether you will move quickly or slowly; whether you will move for extensive changes or limited adjustments; whether you will move by passive resistance or active resistance; or whether you will move at all. The absence of any means might drive one to martyrdom in the hope that this would be a catalyst, starting a chain reaction that would culminate in a mass movement. Here a simple ethical statement is used as a means to power.

A naked illustration of this point is to be found in Trotsky's summary of Lenin's famous April Theses, issued shortly after Lenin's return from exile. Lenin pointed out: "The task of the Bolsheviks is to overthrow the Imperialist Government. But this government rests upon the support of the Social Revolutionaries and Mensheviks, who in turn are supported by the trustfulness of the masses of people. We are in the minority. In these circumstances there can be no talk of violence on our side." The essence of Lenin's speeches during this period was "They have the guns and therefore we are for peace and for reformation through the ballot. When we have the guns then it will be through the bullet." And it was.

Mahatma Gandhi and his use of passive resistance in India presents a striking example of the selection of means. Here, too, we see the inevitable alchemy of time working upon moral equivalents as a consequence of the changing circumstances and positions of the Have-Nots to the Haves, with the natural shift of goals from getting to keeping.

Gandhi is viewed by the world as the epitome of the highest moral behavior with respect to means and ends. We can assume that there are those who would believe that if Gandhi had lived, there would never have been an invasion of Goa or any other armed invasion. Similarly, the politically naive would have regarded it as unbelievable that that great apostle of nonviolence, Nehru, would ever have countenanced the invasion of Goa, for it was Nehru who stated in 1955: "What are the basic elements of our policy in regard to Goa? First, there must be peaceful methods. This is essential unless we give up the roots of all our policies and all our behavior ... We rule out nonpeaceful methods entirely." He was a man committed to nonviolence and ostensibly to the love of mankind, including his enemies. His end was the independence of India from foreign domination, and his means was that of passive resistance. History, and religious and moral opinion, have so enshrined Gandhi in this sacred matrix that in many quarters it is blasphemous to question whether this entire procedure of passive resistance was not simply the only intelligent, realistic, expedient program which Gandhi had at his disposal; and that the "morality" which surrounded this policy of passive resistance was to a large degree a rationale to cloak a pragmatic program with a desired and essential moral cover.

Let us examine this case. First, Gandhi, like any other leader in the field of social action, was compelled to examine the means at hand. If he had had guns he might well have used them in an armed revolution against the British which would have been in keeping with the traditions of revolutions for freedom through force. Gandhi did not have the guns, and if he had had the guns he would not have had the people to use the guns. Gandhi records in his *Autobiography* his astonishment at the passivity and submissiveness of his people in not retaliating or even wanting revenge against the British: "As I proceeded further and further with my inquiry into the atrocities that had been committed on the people, I came across tales of Government's tyranny and the arbitrary despotism of its officers such as I was hardly prepared for, and they filled me with deep pain. What surprised me then, and what still continues to fill me with surprise, was the fact that a province that had furnished the largest number of soldiers to the British Government during the war, should have taken all these brutal excesses lying down."

Gandhi and his associates repeatedly deplored the inability of their people to give organized, effective, violent resistance against injustice and tyranny. His own experience was corroborated by an unbroken series of reiterations from all the leaders of India—that India could not practice physical warfare against her enemies. Many reasons were given, including weakness, lack of arms, having been beaten into submission, and other arguments of a similar nature. Interviewed by Norman Cousins in 1961. Pandit Jawaharlal Nehru described the Hindus of those days as "A demoralized, timid, and hopeless mass bullied and crushed by every dominant interest and incapable of resistance."

Faced with this situation we revert for the moment to Gandhi's assessment and review of the means available to him. It has been stated that if he had had the guns he might have used them; this statement is based on the Declaration of Independence of Mahatma Gandhi issued on January 26, 1930, where he discussed "the fourfold disaster to our country." His fourth indictment against the British reads: "Spiritually, compulsory disarmament has made us unmanly, and the presence of an alien army of occupation, employed with deadly effect to crush in us the spirit of resistance, has made us think we cannot look after ourselves or put up a defense against foreign aggression, or even defend our homes and families . . ." These words more than suggest that if Gandhi had had the weapons for violent resistance and the people to use them this means would not have been so unreservedly rejected as the world would like to think.

On the same point, we might note that once India had secured independence, when Nehru was faced with a dispute with Pakistan over Kashmir, he did not hesitate to use armed force. Now the power arrangements had changed. India had the guns and the trained army to use these

weapons.° Any suggestion that Gandhi would not have
approved the use of violence is negated by Nehru's own
statement in that 1961 interview: "It was a terrible time.
When the news reached me about Kashmir I knew I would
have to act at once—with force. Yet I was greatly troubled
in mind and spirit because I knew we might have to face
a war—so soon after having achieved our independence
through a philosophy of nonviolence. It was horrible to
think of. Yet I acted. Gandhi said nothing to indicate his
disapproval. It was a great relief, I must say. If Gandhi,
the vigorous nonviolent, didn't demur, it made my job a lot

° Reinhold Niebuhr, "British Experience and American Power," *Christianity and Crisis,* Vol. 16, May 14, 1956, page 57:

"The defiance of the United Nations by India on the Kashmir issue
has gone comparatively unobserved. It will be remembered that Kashmir,
a disputed territory, claimed by both Muslim Pakistan and Hindu India,
has a predominately Muslim population but a Hindu ruler. To determine the future political orientation of the area, the United Nations
ordered a plebiscite. Meanwhile, both India and Pakistan refused to move
their troops from the zones which each had previously occupied. Finally,
Nehru took the law into his own hands and annexed the larger part of
Kashmir, which he had shrewdly integrated into the Indian economy. The
Security Council, with only Russia abstaining, unanimously called upon
him to obey the United Nations directive, but the Indian government
refused. Clearly, Nehru does not want a plebiscite now for it would
surely go against India, though he vaguely promises a plebiscite for the
future.

"Morally, the incident puts Nehru in a rather bad light. . . . When
India's vital interests were at stake, Nehru forgot lofty sentiments, sacrificed admirers in the *New Statesman and Nation,* and subjected himself to the charge of inconsistency.

"This policy is either Machiavellian or statesmanlike, according to
your point of view. Our consciences may gag at it, but on the other hand
those eminently moral men, Prime Minister Gladstone of another day
and Secretary Dulles of our day could offer many parallels of policy for
Mr. Nehru, though one may doubt whether either statesman could offer a
coherent analysis of the mixture of modes which entered into the policy.
That is an achievement beyond the competence of very moral men."

easier. This strengthened my view that Gandhi could be adaptable."

Confronted with the issue of what means he could employ against the British, we come to the other criteria previously mentioned; that the kind of means selected and how they can be used is significantly dependent upon the face of the enemy, or the character of his opposition. Gandhi's opposition not only made the effective use of passive resistance possible but practically invited it. His enemy was a British administration characterized by an old, aristocratic, liberal tradition, one which granted a good deal of freedom to its colonials and which always had operated on a pattern of using, absorbing, seducing, or destroying, through flattery or corruption, the revolutionary leaders who arose from the colonial ranks. This was the kind of opposition that would have tolerated and ultimately capitulated before the tactic of passive resistance.

Gandhi's passive resistance would never have had a chance against a totalitarian state such as that of the Nazis. It is dubious whether under those circumstances the idea of passive resistance would even have occurred to Gandhi. It has been pointed out that Gandhi, who was born in 1869, never saw or understood totalitarianism and defined his opposition completely in terms of the character of the British government and what it represented. George Orwell, in his essay *Reflection on Gandhi*, made some pertinent observations on this point: "... He believed in 'arousing the world,' which is only possible if the world gets a chance to hear what you are doing. It is difficult to see how Gandhi's methods could be applied in a country where opponents of the regime disappear in the middle of the night and are never heard of again. Without a free press and the right of assembly it is impossible, not merely to appeal to outside opinion, but to bring a mass movement into being, or even to make your intentions known to your adversary."

From a pragmatic point of view, passive resistance was not only possible, but was the most effective means that could have been selected for the end of ridding India of British control. In organizing, the major negative in the situation has to be converted into the leading positive. In short, knowing that one could not expect violent action from this large and torpid mass, Gandhi organized the inertia: he gave it a goal so that it became purposeful. Their wide familiarity with Dharma made passive resistance no stranger to the Hindustani. To oversimplify, what Gandhi did was to say, "Look, you are all sitting there anyway—so instead of sitting there, why don't you sit over here and while you're sitting, say 'Independence Now!'"

This raises another question about the morality of means and ends. We have already noted that in essence, mankind divides itself into three groups; the Have-Nots, the Have-a-Little, Want-Mores, and the Haves. The purpose of the Haves is to keep what they have. Therefore, the Haves want to maintain the status quo and the Have-Nots to change it. The Haves develop their own morality to justify their means of repression and all other means employed to maintain the status quo. The Haves usually establish laws and judges devoted to maintaining the status quo; since any effective means of changing the status quo are usually illegal and/or unethical in the eyes of the establishment, Have-Nots, from the beginning of time, have been compelled to appeal to "a law higher than man-made law." Then when the Have-Nots achieve success and be-

come the Haves, they are in the position of trying to keep
what they have and their morality shifts with their change
of location in the power pattern.

Eight months after securing independence, the Indian
National Congress outlawed passive resistance and made
it a crime. It was one thing for them to use the means of
passive resistance against the previous Haves, but now in
power they were going to ensure that this means would not
be used against them! No longer as Have-Nots were they
appealing to laws higher than man-made law. Now that
they were making the laws, they were on the side of man-
made laws! Hunger strikes—used so effectively in the revolution—were viewed differently now too. Nehru, in the interview mentioned above, said: "The government will not
be influenced by hunger strikes . . . To tell the truth I
didn't approve of fasting as a political weapon even when
Gandhi practiced it."

Again Sam Adams, the firebrand radical of the American Revolution, provides a clear example. Adams was foremost in proclaiming the right of revolution. However,
following the success of the American Revolution it was
the same Sam Adams who was foremost in demanding the
execution of those Americans who participated in Shays'
Rebellion, charging that no one had a right to engage in
revolution against us!

Moral rationalization is indispensable at all times of
action whether to justify the selection or the use of ends
or means. Machiavelli's blindness to the necessity for moral
clothing to all acts and motives—he said "politics has no
relation to morals"—was his major weakness.

All great leaders, including Churchill, Gandhi, Lincoln,
and Jefferson, always invoked "moral principles" to cover
naked self-interest in the clothing of "freedom," "equality

of mankind," "a law higher than man-made law," and so on. This even held under circumstances of national crises when it was universally assumed that the end justified any means. *All effective actions require the passport of morality.*

The examples are everywhere. In the United States the rise of the civil rights movement in the late 1950s was marked by the use of passive resistance in the South against segregation. Violence in the South would have been suicidal; political pressure was then impossible; the only recourse was economic pressure with a few fringe activities. Legally blocked by state laws, hostile police and courts, they were compelled like all Have-Nots from time immemorial to appeal to "a law higher than man-made law." In his *Social Contract,* Rousseau noted the obvious, that "Law is a very good thing for men with property and a very bad thing for men without property." Passive resistance remained one of the few means available to anti-segregationist forces until they had secured the voting franchise in fact. Furthermore, passive resistance was also a good defensive tactic since it curtailed the opportunities for use of the power resources of the status quo for forcible repression. Passive resistance was chosen for the same pragmatic reason that all tactics are selected. But it assumes the necessary moral and religious adornments.

However, when passive resistance becomes massive and threatening it gives birth to violence. Southern Negroes have no tradition of Dharma, and are close enough to their Northern compatriots so that contrasting conditions between the North and the South are a visible as well as a constant spur. Add to this the fact that the Southern poor whites do not operate by British tradition but reflect generations of violence; the future does not argue for making a special religion of nonviolence. It will be remembered for what it was, the best tactic for its time and place.

As more effective means become available, the Negro civil rights movement will divest itself of these decorations and substitute a new moral philosophy in keeping with its new means and opportunities. The explanation will be, as it always has been, "Times have changed." This is happening today.

The eleventh rule of the ethics of means and ends is that goals must be phrased in general terms like "Liberty, Equality, Fraternity," "Of the Common Welfare," "Pursuit of Happiness," or "Bread and Peace." Whitman put it: "The goal once named cannot be countermanded." It has been previously noted that the wise man of action knows that frequently in the stream of action of means towards ends, whole new and unexpected ends are among the major results of the action. From a Civil War fought as a means to preserve the Union came the end of slavery.

In this connection, it must be remembered that history is made up of actions in which one end results in other ends. Repeatedly, scientific discoveries have resulted from experimental research committed to ends or objectives that have little relationship with the discoveries. Work on a seemingly minor practical program has resulted in feedbacks of major creative basic ideas. J. C. Flugel notes, in *Man, Morals and Society*, that ". . . In psychology, too, we have no right to be astonished if, while dealing with a means (e.g., the cure of a neurotic symptom, the discovery of more efficient ways of learning, or the relief of industrial fatigue) we find that we have modified our attitude toward the end (acquired some new insight into the nature of mental health, the role of education, or the place of work in human life)."

The mental shadow boxing on the subject of means and ends is typical of those who are the observers and not the actors in the battlefields of life. In *The Yogi and the Commissar,* Koestler begins with the basic fallacy of an arbitrary demarcation between *expediency* and *morality*; between the Yogi for whom the end never justifies the means and the Commissar for whom the end always justifies the means. Koestler attempts to extricate himself from this self-constructed strait jacket by proposing that the end justifies the means only within narrow limits. Here Koestler, even in an academic confrontation with action, was compelled to take the first step in the course of compromise on the road to action and power. How "narrow" the limits and who defines the "narrow" limits opens the door to the premises discussed here. The kind of personal safety and security sought by the advocates of the sanctity of means and ends lies only in the womb of Yogism or the monastery, and even there it is darkened by the repudiation of that moral principle that they are their brothers' keepers.

Bertrand Russell, in his *Human Society in Ethics and Politics,* observed that "Morality is so much concerned with means that it seems almost immoral to consider anything solely in relation to its intrinsic worth. But obviously nothing has any value as a means unless that to which it is a means has value on its own account. It follows that intrinsic value is logically prior to value as means."

The organizer, the revolutionist, the activist or call him what you will, who is committed to a free and open society is in that commitment anchored to a complex of high values. These values include the basic morals of all organized religions; their base is the preciousness of human life. These values include freedom, equality, justice, peace, the right to dissent; the values that were the banners of hope and yearning of all revolutions of men, whether the French Revolution's "Liberty, Fraternity, Equality," the Russians' "Bread and Peace," the brave Spanish people's "Better to die on your feet than to live on your knees," or our Revolution's "No Taxation Without Representation." They include the values in our own Bill of Rights. If a state voted for school segregation or a community organization voted to keep blacks out, and claimed justification by virtue of the "democratic process," then this violation of the value of equality would have converted democracy into a prostitute. Democracy is not an end; it is the best political means available toward the achievement of these values.

Means and ends are so qualitatively interrelated that the true question has never been the proverbial one, "Does the End justify the Means?" but always has been "Does this *particular* end justify this *particular* means?"

A Word
About Words

THE PASSIONS OF MANKIND have boiled over into all areas of political life, including its vocabulary. The words most common in politics have become stained with human hurts, hopes, and frustrations. All of them are loaded with popular opprobrium, and their use results in a conditioned, negative, emotional response. Even the word *politics* itself, which Webster says is "the science and art of government," is generally viewed in a context of corruption. Ironically, the dictionary synonyms are "discreet; provident, diplomatic, wise."

The same discolorations attach to other words prevalent in the language of politics, words like *power, self-interest, compromise*, and *conflict*. They become twisted and warped, viewed as evil. Nowhere is the prevailing political illiteracy more clearly revealed than in these typical interpretations of words. This is why we pause here for a word about words.

POWER

The question may legitimately be raised, why not use
other words—words that mean the same but are peaceful,
and do not result in such negative emotional reactions?
There are a number of fundamental reasons for rejecting
such substitution. First, by using combinations of words
such as "harnessing the energy" instead of the single word
"power," we begin to dilute the meaning; and as we use
purifying synonyms, we dissolve the bitterness, the an-
guish, the hate and love, the agony and the triumph at-
tached to these words, leaving an aseptic imitation of life.
In the politics of life we are concerned with the slaves and
the Caesars, not the vestal virgins. It is not just that, in communication as in thought, we must ever strive toward
simplicity. (The masterpieces of philosophic or scientific
statement are frequently no longer than a few words, for
example, "$E = mc^2$.") It is more than that: it is a determination not to detour around reality.

To use any other word but power is to change the
meaning of everything we are talking about. As Mark
Twain once put it, "The difference between the right word
and the almost-right word is the difference between lightning and the lightning bug."

Power is the right word just as self-interest, compromise, and the other simple political words are, for they
were conceived in and have become part of politics from
the beginning of time. To pander to those who have no
stomach for straight language, and insist upon bland, non-
controversial sauces, is a waste of time. They cannot or

deliberately will not understand what we are discussing here. I agree with Nietzsche's statement in *The Genealogy of Morals* on this point:

> Why stroke the hypersensitive ears of our modern weaklings? Why yield even a single step . . . to the Tartuffery of words? For us psychologists that would involve a Tartuffery of *action* . . . For a psychologist today shows his good taste (others may say his integrity) in this, if in anything, that he resists the shamefully *moralized* manner of speaking which makes all modern judgments about men and things slimy.

We approach a critical point when our tongues trap our minds. I do not propose to be trapped by tact at the expense of truth. Striving to avoid the force, vigor, and simplicity of the word "power," we soon become averse to thinking in vigorous, simple, honest terms. We strive to invent sterilized synonyms, cleansed of the opprobrium of the word *power*—but the new words mean something different, so that they tranquilize us, begin to shepherd our mental processes off the main, conflict-ridden, grimy, and realistic power-paved highway of life. To travel down the sweeter-smelling, peaceful, more socially acceptable, more respectable, indefinite byways, ends in a failure to achieve an honest understanding of the issues that we must come to grips with if we are to do the job.

Let us look at the word *power*. Power, meaning "ability, whether physical, mental, or moral, to act," has become an evil word, with overtones and undertones that suggest the sinister, the unhealthy, the Machiavellian. It suggests a phantasmagoria of the nether regions. The moment the word *power* is mentioned it is as though hell had been opened, exuding the stench of the devil's cesspool of corruption. It evokes images of cruelty, dishonesty, selfishness, arrogance, dictatorship, and abject suffering. The word *power* is associated with conflict; it is unacceptable in our present Madison Avenue deodorized hygiene, where controversy is blasphemous and the value is being liked and not offending others. Power, in our minds, has become almost synonymous with corruption and immorality.

Whenever the word *power* is mentioned, somebody sooner or later will refer to the classical statement of Lord Acton and cite it as follows: "Power corrupts, and absolute power corrupts absolutely." In fact the correct quotation is: "Power *tends* to corrupt, and absolute power corrupts absolutely." We can't even read Acton's statement accurately, our minds are so confused by our conditioning.

The corruption of power is not in power, but in ourselves. And yet, what is this power which men live by and to a significant degree live for? Power is the very essence, the dynamo of life. It is the power of the heart pumping blood and sustaining life in the body. It is the power of active citizen participation pulsing upward, providing a unified strength for a common purpose. Power is an essential life force always in operation, either changing the world or opposing change. Power, or organized energy, may be a man-killing explosive or a life-saving drug. The power of a gun may be used to enforce slavery, or to achieve freedom.

The power of the human brain can create man's most glorious achievements, and develop perspectives and insights into the nature of life-opening horizons previously beyond the imagination. The power of the human mind can also devise philosophies and ways of life that are most destructive for the future of mankind. Either way, power is the dynamo of life.

Alexander Hamilton, in *The Federalist Papers*, put it this way: "What is a power, but the ability or faculty of doing a thing? What is the ability to do a thing, but the power of employing the *means* necessary to its execution?" Pascal, who was definitely not a cynic, observed that: "Justice without power is impotent; power without justice is tyranny." St. Ignatius, the founder of the Jesuit order, did not shrink from the recognition of power when he issued his dictum: "To do a thing well a man needs power and competence." We could call the roll of all who have played their parts in history and find the word *power*, not a substitute word, used in their speech and writings.

It is impossible to conceive of a world devoid of power; the only choice of concepts is between organized and unorganized power. Mankind has progressed only through learning how to develop and organize instruments of power in order to achieve order, security, morality, and civilized life itself, instead of a sheer struggle for physical survival. Every organization known to man, from government down, has had only one reason for being—that is, organization for power in order to put into practice or promote its common purpose.

When we talk about a person's "lifting himself by his own bootstraps" we are talking about power. Power must be understood for what it is, for the part it plays in every area of our life, if we are to understand it and thereby grasp the essentials of relationships and functions between groups and organizations, particularly in a pluralistic society. *To know power and not fear it is essential to its con-*

structive use and control. In short, life without power is death; a world without power would be a ghostly waste-land, a dead planet!

SELF-INTEREST

Self-interest, like *power,* wears the black shroud of nega-tivism and suspicion. To many the synonym for self-inter-est is selfishness. The word is associated with a repugnant conglomeration of vices such as narrowness, self-seeking, and self-centeredness, everything that is opposite to the virtues of altruism and selflessness. This common defini-tion is contrary, of course, to our everyday experiences, as well as to the observations of all great students of politics and life. The myth of altruism as a motivating factor in our behavior could arise and survive only in a society bundled in the sterile gauze of New England puritanism and Protestant morality and tied together with the ribbons of Madison Avenue public relations. It is one of the classic American fairy tales.

From the great teachers of Judaeo-Christian morality and the philosophers, to the economists, and to the wise observers of the politics of man, there has always been universal agreement on the part that self-interest plays as a prime moving force in man's behavior. The importance of self-interest has never been challenged; it has been accepted as an inevitable fact of life. In the words of Christ, "Greater love has no man than this, that a man lay down his life for his friends." Aristotle said, in *Politics,* "Everyone thinks chiefly of his own, hardly ever of the public interest." Adam Smith, in *The Wealth of Nations*, noted that "It is not from the benevolence of the butcher, the brewer, or the baker that we expect our dinner, but from their regard of their own interest. We address ourselves not to their humanity, but to their self-love, and never talk to them of our own necessities, but of their advantage." In all the reasoning found in *The Federalist Papers,* no point is so central and agreed upon as "Rich and poor alike are prone to act upon impulse rather than pure reason and to narrow conceptions of self-interest . . ." To question the force of self-interest that pervades all areas of political life is to refuse to see man as he is, to see him only as we would like him to be.

And yet, next to this acceptance of self-interest, there are certain observations I would like to make. Machiavelli, with whom the idea of self-interest seems to have gained its greatest notoriety, at least among those who are unaware of the tradition, said:

> This is to be asserted in general of men, that they are ungrateful, fickle, fake, cowardly, covetous, as long as you succeed they are yours entirely; they will offer you their blood, property, life, and children when the need is far distant; but when it approaches they turn against you.

But Machiavelli makes a mortal mistake when he rules out the "moral" factors of politics and holds purely to self-interest as he defines it. This mistake can only be accounted for on the basis that Machiavelli's experience as an active politician was not too great, for otherwise he could not have overlooked the obvious fluidity of every man's self-interest. The overall case must be of larger dimensions than that of self-interest narrowly defined; it must be large enough to include and provide for the shifting dimensions of self-interest. You may appeal to one self-interest to get me to the battlefront to fight; but once I am there, my prime self-interest becomes to stay alive, and if we are victorious my self-interest may, and usually does, dictate entirely unexpected goals rather than those I had before the war. For example, the United States in World War II fervently allied with Russia against Germany, Japan, and Italy, and shortly after victory fervently allied with its former enemies—Germany, Japan, and Italy—against its former ally, the U.S.S.R.

These drastic shifts of self-interest can be rationalized only under a huge, limitless umbrella of general "moral" principles such as liberty, justice, freedom, a law higher than man-made law, and so on. Morality, so-called, becomes the continuum as self-interests shift.

Within this morality there appears to be a tearing conflict, probably due to the layers of inhibition in our kind of moralistic civilization—it appears shameful to admit that we operate on the basis of naked self-interest, so we desperately try to reconcile every shift of circumstances that is to our self-interest in terms of a broad moral justification or rationalization. With one breath we point out that we are utterly opposed to communism, but that we love the Russian people (loving people is in keeping with the tenets of our civilization). What we hate is the atheism and the suppression of the individual that we attribute as characteristics substantiating the "immorality" of communism. On this we base our powerful opposition. We do not admit the actual fact: our own self-interest.

We proclaimed all of these negative, diabolical Russian characteristics just prior to the Nazi invasion of Russia. The Soviets were then the cynical despots who

connived in the non-aggression pact with Hitler, the ruth-
less invaders who brought disaster to the Poles and the
Finns. They were a people in chains and in misery, held
in slavery by a dictator's might; they were a people whose
rulers so distrusted them that the Red Army was not permitted to have live ammunition because they might turn
their guns against the Kremlin. All this was our image. But
within minutes of the invasion of Russia by the Nazis,
when self-interest dictated that the defeat of Russia would
be disastrous to our interest, then—suddenly—they became
the gallant, great, warm, loving Russian people; the dictator became the benevolent and loving Uncle Joe; the
Red Army soon was filled with trust and devotion to its
government, fighting with an unparalleled bravery and
employing a scorched-earth policy against the enemy. The
Russian allies certainly had God on their side—after all,
He was on ours. Our June, 1941, shift was more dramatic
and sudden than our shift against the Russians shortly
after the defeat of our common enemy. In both cases our
self-interest was disguised, as the banners of freedom,
liberty, and decency were unveiled—first against the
Nazis, and six years later against the Russians.

In our present relationship with Tito and the Yugo-
slavian communists, then, the issue is not that Tito represents communism, but that he is not part of the Russian
power alignment. Here we take the position we took after
the Nazi invasion, where suddenly communism became,
"Well, after all, it's their way of life and we believe in the
right of self-determination and it's up to the Russians to
have the government they like," *as long as they are on our
side and do not threaten our self-interest.* Too, there is no
question that, with all our denunciation of the Red Chinese, if they announced that they were no longer a part of

the world communist conspiracy or alignment of forces,
they would be overnight acceptable to us, acclaimed by us,
and provided with all kinds of aid, just so long as they were
on our side. In essence, what we are saying is that we do
not care what kind of a communist you are so long as you
do not threaten our self-interest.

> Let me give you an example of what I mean
> by some of the differences between the world as
> it is and the world as we would like it to be.
> Recently, after lecturing at Stanford University,
> I met a Soviet professor of political economics
> from the University of Leningrad. The opening
> of our conversation was illustrative of the defini-
> tions and outlook of those who live in the world
> as it is. The Russian began by asking me, "Where
> do you stand on communism?" I replied, "That's
> a bad question since the real question is, assum-
> ing both of us are operating in and thinking of
> the world as it is, 'Whose Communists are they—
> yours or ours?' If they are ours, then we are all
> for them. If they are yours, obviously we are
> against them. Communism itself is irrelevant.
> The issue is whether they are on our side or yours.
> Now, if you Russians didn't have a first mortgage
> on Castro, we would be talking about Cuba's
> right to self-determination and the fact that you
> couldn't have a free election until after there had
> been a period of education following the repres-
> sion of the dictatorship of Batista. As a matter of
> fact, if you should start trying to push for a free
> election in Yugoslavia, we might even send over
> our Marines to prevent this kind of sabotage. The
> same goes if you should try to do it in Formosa."
> The Russian came back with, "What is your defi-
> nition of a free election outside of your country?"
> I said, "Well, our definition of a free election in,
> say, Vietnam is pretty much what your definition

is in your satellites—if we've got everything so
set that we are going to win, then it's a free election. Otherwise, it's bloody terrorism! Isn't that
your definition?" The Russian's reaction was,
"Well, yes, more or less!"

—Saul D. Alinsky, *Reveille for Radicals,* Random
House, Vintage Books, New York, rev. 1969,
p. 227.

We repeatedly get caught in this conflict between our
professed moral principles and the real reasons why we do
things—to wit, our self-interest. We are always able to
mask those real reasons in words of beneficent goodness—
freedom, justice, and so on. Such tears as appear in the
fabric of this moral masquerade sometimes embarrass us.

It is interesting that the communists do not seem to
concern themselves with these moral justifications for their
naked acts of self-interest. In a way, this becomes embarrassing too; it makes us feel that they may be laughing
at us, knowing well that we are motivated by self-interest
too, but are determined to disguise it. We feel that they
may be laughing at us as they struggle in the sea of world
politics, stripped to their shorts, while we flop around,
fully dressed in our white tie and tails.

And yet with all this there is that wondrous quality
of man that from time to time floods over the natural dams
of survival and self-interest. We witnessed it in the summer of 1964 when white college students risked their lives
to carry the torch of human freedom into darkest Missis-
sippi. An earlier instance: George Orwell describes his
self-interest in entering the trenches during the Spanish
Civil War as a matter of trying to stop the spreading horror of fascism. Yet once he was in the trenches, his self-
interest changed to the goal of getting out alive. Still, I

have no question that if Orwell had been given a military assignment from which he could easily have got lost, he would not have wandered to the rear at the price of jeopardizing the lives of some of his comrades; he would never have pursued his "self-interest." These are the exceptions to the rule, but there have been enough of them flashing through the murky past of history to suggest that these episodic transfigurations of the human spirit are more than the flash of fireflies.

COMPROMISE

Compromise is another word that carries shades of weakness, vacillation, betrayal of ideals, surrender of moral principles. In the old culture, when virginity was a virtue, one referred to a woman's being "compromised." The word is generally regarded as ethically unsavory and ugly.

But to the organizer, compromise is a key and beautiful word. It is always present in the pragmatics of operation. It is making the deal, getting that vital breather, usually the victory. If you start with nothing, demand 100 per cent, then compromise for 30 per cent, you're 30 per cent ahead.

A free and open society is an on-going conflict, interrupted periodically by compromises—which then become the start for the continuation of conflict, compromise, and on ad infinitum. Control of power is based on compromise in our Congress and among the executive, legislative, and judicial branches. A society devoid of compromise is totalitarian. If I had to define a free and open society in one word, the word would be "compromise."

EGO

All definitions of words, like everything else, are relative. Definition is to a major degree dependent upon your partisan position. Your leader is always flexible, he has pride in the dignity of his cause, he is unflinching, sincere, an ingenious tactician fighting the good fight. To the opposition he is unprincipled and will go whichever way the wind blows, his arrogance is masked by a fake humility, he is dogmatically stubborn, a hypocrite, unscrupulous and unethical, and he will do anything to win; he is leading the forces of evil. To one side he is a demigod, to the other a demagogue.

Nowhere is the relativity of a definition more germane in the arena of life than the word *ego*. Anyone who is working against the Haves is always facing odds, and in many cases heavy odds. If he or she does not have that complete self-confidence (or call it ego) that he can win, then the battle is lost before it is even begun. I have seen so-called trained organizers go out to another city with an assignment of organizing a community of approximately 100,000 people, take one look and promptly wire in a resignation. To be able to look at a community of people and say to yourself, "I will organize them in so many weeks," "I will take on the corporations, the press and anything else," is to be a real organizer.

"Ego," as we understand and use it here, cannot be even vaguely confused with, nor is it remotely related to, egotism. No would-be organizer afflicted with egotism can avoid hiding this from the people with whom he is working, no contrived humility can conceal it. Nothing antagonizes people and alienates them from a would-be organizer more than the revealing flashes of arrogance, vanity, impatience, and contempt of a personal egotism.

The ego of the organizer is stronger and more monumental than the ego of the leader. The leader is driven by the desire for power, while the organizer is driven by the desire to create. The organizer is in a true sense reaching for the highest level for which man can reach—to create, to be a "great creator," to play God.

An infection of egotism would make it impossible to respect the dignity of individuals, to understand people, or to strive to develop the other elements that make up the ideal organizer. Egotism is mainly a defensive reaction of feelings of personal inadequacy—ego is a positive conviction and belief in one's ability, with no need for egotistical behavior.

Ego moves on every level. How can an organizer respect the dignity of an individual if he does not respect his own dignity? How can he believe in people if he does not really believe in himself? How can he convince people that they have it within themselves, that they have the power to stand up to win, if he does not believe it of himself? Ego must be so all-pervading that the personality of the organizer is contagious, that it converts the people from despair to defiance, creating a mass ego.

CONFLICT

Conflict is another bad word in the general opinion. This is a consequence of two influences in our society: one influence is organized religion, which has espoused a rhetoric of "turning the other cheek" and has quoted the Scriptures as the devil never would have dared because of their major previous function of supporting the Establishment. The second influence is probably the most subversive and insidious one, and it has permeated the American scene in the last generation: that is Madison Avenue public relations, middle-class moral hygiene, which has made of conflict or controversy something negative and undesirable. This has all been part of an Advertising Culture that emphasizes getting along with people and avoiding friction. If you look at our television commercials you get the picture that American society is largely devoted to ensuring that no odors come from our mouths or armpits. Consensus is a keynote—one must not offend one's fellow man; and so today we find that people in the mass media are fired for expressing their opinions or being "controversial"; in the churches they are fired for the same reason but the words used there are "lacking in prudence"; and on university campuses, faculty members are fired for the same reason, but the words used there are "personality difficulties."

Conflict is the essential core of a free and open society. If one were to project the democratic way of life in the form of a musical score, its major theme would be the harmony of dissonance.

The Education of
an Organizer

THE BUILDING of many mass power organizations to merge into a national popular power force cannot come without many organizers. Since organizations are created, in large part, by the organizer, we must find out what creates the organizer. This has been the major problem of my years of organizational experience: the finding of potential organizers and their training. For the past two years I have had a special training school for organizers with a full-time, fifteen-month program.

Its students have ranged from middle-class women activists to Catholic priests and Protestant ministers of all denominations, from militant Indians to Chicanos to Puerto Ricans to blacks from all parts of the black power spectrum, from Panthers to radical philosophers, from a variety of campus activists, S.D.S. and others, to a priest who was joining a revolutionary party in South America. Geographically they have come from campuses and Jesuit seminaries in Boston to Chicanos from tiny Texas towns, middle-class people from Chicago and Hartford and Seattle, and almost every place in between. An increasing number of students come from Canada, from the Indians of the northwest to the middle class of the Maritime Provinces. For years before the formal school was begun, I spent most of my time on the education as an organizer of every member of my staff.

The education of an organizer requires frequent long conferences on organizational problems, analysis of power patterns, communication, conflict tactics, the education and development of community leaders, and the methods of introduction of new issues. In these discussions, we have found ourselves dealing with quite a range of issues: internal problems of a clique in a Los Angeles organization out to get rid of its organizer; a Christmas tree selling fundraising fiasco in San Jose and why it failed; a massive voter registration drive in a Chicago project which was being delayed in getting started; a group in Rochester, New York, attacking the organizer so that they could get their hot hands on the funds earmarked for organization—and so on.

Always the potential organizer's personal experience was used as the basis for teaching. Always after the problem was solved there would be long sessions in which a postmortem would dissect the specifics and then stitch them into a synthesis, a body of concepts. All experiences are significant only insofar as they are related to and illuminating a central concept. History does not repeat specific situations—if any of the examples in these pages are read isolated from the general concept, they will be nothing more than a series of anecdotes. Everything became a learning experience.

Frequently personal domestic hangups were part of the conferences. An organizer's working schedule is so

continuous that time is meaningless; meetings and cau-
cuses drag endlessly into the early morning hours; any
schedule is marked by constant unexpected unscheduled
meetings; work pursues an organizer into his or her home,
so that either he is on the phone or there are people drop-
ping in. The marriage record of organizers is with rare
exception disastrous. Further, the tensions, the hours, the
home situation, and the opportunities, do not argue for
fidelity. Also, with rare exception, I have not known really
competent organizers who were concerned about celibacy.
Here and there are wives and husbands or those in love
relationships who understand and are committed to the
work, and are real sources of strength to the organizer.

Besides the full-timers, there were the community
leaders whom we trained on the job to be organizers. Organizers are not only essential to start and build an
organization; they are also essential to keep it going.
Maintaining interest and activity, keeping the group's
goals strong and flexible at once, is a different operation
but still organization.

As I look back on the results of those years, they seem
to be a potpourri, with, I would judge, more failures than
successes. Here and there are organizers who are outstanding in their chosen fields and are featured by the press
as my trained "protégés," but to me the overall record
has been unpromising.

Those out of their local communities who were
trained on the job achieved certain levels and were at the
end of their line. If one thinks of an organizer as a highly
imaginative and creative architect and engineer then the
best we have been able to train on the job were skilled
plumbers, electricians, and carpenters, all essential to the

building and maintenance of their community structure but incapable of going elsewhere to design and execute a new structure in a new community.

Then there were others who learned to be outstanding organizers in particular kinds of communities with particular ethnic groups but in a different scene with different ethnic groups couldn't organize their way out of a paper bag.

Then there were those rare campus activists who could organize a substantial number of students—but they were utter failures when it came to trying to communicate with and organize lower-middle-class workers.

Labor union organizers turned out to be poor community organizers. Their experience was tied to a pattern of fixed points, whether it was definite demands on wages, pensions, vacation periods, or other working conditions, and all of this was anchored into particular contract dates. Once the issues were settled and a contract signed, the years before the next contract negotiation held only grievance meetings about charges on contract violations by either side. Mass organization is a different animal, it is not housebroken. There are no fixed chronological points or definite issues. The demands are always changing; the situation is fluid and ever-shifting; and many of the goals are not in concrete terms of dollars and hours but are psychological and constantly changing, like "such stuff as dreams are made on." I have seen labor organizers almost out of their minds from the community organization scene.

When labor leaders have talked about organizing the poor, their talk has been based on nostalgia, a wistful look back to the labor organizers of the C.I.O. through the great depression of the thirties. Those "labor organizers" —Powers Hapgood, Henry Johnson, and Lee Pressman, for instance—were primarily middle-class revolutionary activists to whom the C.I.O. labor organizing drive was just one of many activities. The agendas of those labor union mass meetings were 10 per cent on the specific problems of that union and 90 per cent speakers on the conditions and needs of the southern Okies, the Spanish Civil War and the International Brigade, raising funds for blacks who were on trial in some southern state, demanding higher relief for the unemployed, denouncing police brutality, raising funds for anti-Nazi organizations, demanding an end to American sales of scrap iron to the Japanese military complex, and on and on. They were radicals, and they were good at their job: they organized vast sectors of middle-class America in support of their programs. But they are gone, now, and any resemblance between them and the present professional labor organizer is only in title.

Among the organizers I trained and failed with, there were some who memorized the words and the related experiences and concepts. Listening to them was like listening to a tape playing back my presentation word for word. Clearly there was little understanding; clearly, they could not do more than elementary organization. The problem with so many of them was and is their failure to understand that a statement of a specific situation is significant only in its relationship to and its illumination of a general concept. Instead they see the specific action as a terminal point. They find it difficult to grasp the fact that no situation ever repeats itself, that no tactic can be precisely the same.

Then there were those who had trained in schools of social work to become community organizers. Community organization 101, 102, and 103. They had done "field work" and acquired even a specialized vocabulary. They call it "C.O." (which to us means Conscientious Objector) or "Community Org." (which to us evokes a huge Freudian fantasy). Basically the difference between their goals and ours is that they organize to get rid of four-legged rats and stop there; we organize to get rid of four-legged rats so we can get on to removing two-legged rats. Among those who, disillusioned, reject the formalized garbage they learned in school, the odds are heavily against their developing into effective organizers. One reason is that despite their verbal denunciations of their past training there is a strong subconscious block against repudiating two to three years of life spent in this training, as well as the financial cost of these courses.

Through these years I have constantly tried to search out reasons for our failures as well as our occasional successes in training organizers. Our teaching methods, those of others, our personal competency for teaching, and improvised new teaching approaches, have and are being examined; our own self-criticism is far more rigorous than that of our most bitter critics. All of us have faults. I know that in a community, working as an organizer, I have unlimited patience in talking to and listening to the local residents. Any organizer must have this patience. But among my faults is that in a teaching position at the training institute or at conferences I become an intellectual snob with unimaginative, limited students, impatient, bored, and inexcusably rude.

I have improvised teaching approaches. For example, knowing that one can only communicate and understand in terms of one's experience, we had to construct experience for our students. Most people do not accumulate a body of experience. Most people go through life undergoing a series of happenings, which pass through their systems undigested. Happenings become experiences when they are digested, when they are reflected on, related to general patterns, and synthesized.

There is meaning to that cliché, "We learn from experience." Our job was to shovel those happenings back into the student's system so he could digest them into experience. During a seminar I would say, "Life is the expectation of the unexpected—the things you worry about rarely happen. Something new, the unexpected, will usually come in from outside the ball park. You're all nodding as if you understand but you really don't. What I've said are just words to you. I want you to go to your private cubbyholes and think for the next four hours. Try to remember all the things you worried about during the last years and whether they ever happened or what did happen —and then we'll talk about it."

At the next session the student reactions were excited, "Hey, you're right. Only one out of the eight big worries I've had ever happened—and even that one was different from the way I worried about it. I understand what you mean." And he did.

While the experience of trying to educate organizers has been nowhere so successful as I'd hoped, there was a great deal of education for me and my associates. We were constantly in a state of self-examination. First, we learned what the qualities of an ideal organizer are; and second, we were confronted with a basic question: whether it was possible to teach or educate for the achieving of these qualities.

The area of experience and communication is fundamental to the organizer. An organizer can communicate only within the areas of experience of his audience; otherwise there is no communication. The organizer, in his constant hunt for patterns, universalities, and meaning, is always building up a body of experience.

Through his imagination he is constantly moving in on the happenings of others, identifying with them and extracting their happenings into his own mental digestive system and thereby accumulating more experience. It is essential for communication that he know of their experiences. Since one can communicate only through the experiences of the other, it becomes clear that the organizer begins to develop an abnormally large body of experience.

He learns the local legends, anecdotes, values, idioms. He listens to small talk. He refrains from rhetoric foreign to the local culture: he knows that worn-out words like "white racist," "fascist pig," and "motherfucker" have been so spewed about that using them is now within the negative experience of the local people, serving only to identify the speaker as "one of those nuts" and to turn off any further communication.

And yet the organizer must not try to fake it. He must be himself. I remember a first meeting with Mexican-American leaders in a California barrio where they served me a special Mexican dinner. When we were halfway through I put down my knife and fork saying, "My God! Do you eat this stuff because you like it or because you have to? I think it's as lousy as the Jewish kosher crap I had to eat as a kid!" There was a moment of shocked silence and then everybody roared. Suddenly barriers began to come down as they all began talking and laughing. They were so accustomed to the Anglo who would rave about the beauty of Mexican food even though they knew it was killing him, the Anglo who had memorized a few Spanish phrases with the inevitable *hasta la vista*, that it was a refreshingly honest experience to them. The incident became a legend to many and you would hear them say, for instance, "He has as much use for that guy as Alinsky has for Mexican food." A number of the Mexican-Americans present confessed that they only ate some of those dishes when they entertained an Anglo. The same faking goes on with whites on certain items of blacks' "soul food."

There is a difference between honesty and rude disrespect of another's tradition. The organizer will err far less by being himself than by engaging in "professional techniques" when the people really know better. It shows respect for people to be honest, as in the Mexican dinner episode; they are being treated as people and not guinea pigs being techniqued. It is most important that this action be understood in context. Prior to my remark there had been a warm personal discussion of the problems of the people. They knew not only of my concern about their plight but that I liked them as people. I felt their response in friendship, and we were together. It is in this totality of the situation that I did what, otherwise, would have been offensive.

The qualities we were trying to develop in organizers in the years of attempting to train them included some qualities that in all probability cannot be taught. They either had them, or could get them only through a miracle from above or below. Other qualities they might have as potentials that could be developed. Sometimes the development of one quality triggered off unsuspected others. I learned to check against the list and spot the negatives; and if it was impossible to develop that quality, at least I could be aware and on guard to try to diminish its negative effect upon the work.

Here is the list of the ideal elements of an organizer —the items one looks for in identifying potential organizers and in appraising the future possibilities of new organizers, and the pivot points of any kind of educational curricula for organizers. Certainly it is an idealized list— I doubt that such qualities, in such intensity, ever come together in one man or woman; yet the best of organizers should have them all, to a strong extent, and any organizer needs at least a degree of each.

Curiosity. What makes an organizer organize? He is driven by a compulsive curiosity that knows no limits. Warning clichés such as "curiosity killed a cat" are meaningless to him, for life is for him a search for a pattern, for similarities in seeming differences, for differences in seeming similarities, for an order in the chaos about us, for a meaning to the life around him and its relationship to his own life—and the search never ends. He goes forth with the question as his mark, and suspects that there are no answers, only further questions. The organizer becomes a carrier of the contagion of curiosity, for a people asking "why" are beginning to rebel. The questioning of the hitherto accepted ways and values is the reformation stage that precedes and is so essential to the revolution.

Here, I couldn't disagree more with Freud. In a letter to Marie Bonaparte, he said, "The moment a man questions the meaning and value of life, he is sick." If there is, somewhere, an answer about life, I suspect that the key to it is finding the core question.

Actually, Socrates was an organizer. The function of an organizer is to raise questions that agitate, that break through the accepted pattern. Socrates, with his goal of "know thyself," was raising the internal questions within the individual that are so essential for the revolution which is external to the individual. So Socrates was carrying out the first stage of making revolutionaries. If he had been permitted to continue raising questions about the meaning of life, to examine life and refuse the conventional values, the internal revolution would soon have moved out into the political arena. Those who tried him and sentenced him to death knew what they were doing.

Irreverence. Curiosity and irreverence go together. Curiosity cannot exist without the other. Curiosity asks, "Is this true?" "Just because this has always been the way, is this the best or right way of life, the best or right religion, political or economic value, morality?" To the questioner nothing is sacred. He detests dogma, defies any finite definition of morality, rebels against any repression of a free, open search for ideas no matter where they may lead. He is challenging, insulting, agitating, discrediting. He stirs unrest. As with all life, this is a paradox, for his irreverence is rooted in a deep reverence for the enigma of life, and an incessant search for its meaning. It could be argued that reverence for others, for their freedom from injustice, poverty, ignorance, exploitation, discrimination, disease, war, hate, and fear, is not a necessary quality in a successful organizer. All I can say is that such reverence is a quality I would have to see in anyone I would undertake to teach.

Imagination. Imagination is the inevitable partner of irreverence and curiosity. How can one be curious without being imaginative?

According to Webster's Unabridged, imagination is the "mental synthesis of new ideas from elements experienced separately . . . The broader meaning . . . starts with the notion of mental imaging of things suggested but not previously experienced, and thence expands . . . to the idea of mental creation and poetic idealization [creative imagination] . . ." To the organizer, imagination is not only all this but something deeper. It is the dynamism that starts and sustains him in his whole life of action as an organizer. It ignites and feeds the force that drives him to organize for change.

There was a time when I believed that the basic quality that an organizer needed was a deep sense of anger against injustice and that this was the prime motivation that kept him going. I now know that it is something else: this abnormal imagination that sweeps him into a close identification with mankind and projects him into its plight. He suffers with them and becomes angry at the injustice and begins to organize the rebellion. Clarence Darrow put it on more of a self-interest basis: "I had a vivid imagination. Not only could I put myself in the other person's place, but I could not avoid doing so. My sympathies always went out to the weak, the suffering, and the poor. Realizing their sorrows I tried to relieve them in order that I myself might be relieved."

Imagination is not only the fuel for the force that keeps organizers organizing, it is also the basis for effective tactics and action. The organizer knows that the real action is in the reaction of the opposition. To realistically appraise and anticipate the probable reactions of the enemy, he must be able to identify with them, too, in his imagination, and foresee their reactions to his actions.

A sense of humor. Back to Webster's Unabridged: humor is defined as "The mental faculty of discovering, expressing, or appreciating ludicrous or absurdly incongruous elements in ideas, situations, happenings, or acts . . ." or "A changing and uncertain state of mind . . ."

The organizer, searching with a free and open mind

void of certainty, hating dogma, finds laughter not just a way to maintain his sanity but also a key to understanding life. Essentially, life is a tragedy; and the converse of tragedy is comedy. One can change a few lines in any Greek tragedy and it becomes a comedy, and vice versa. Knowing that contradictions are the signposts of progress he is ever on the alert for contradictions. A sense of humor helps him identify and make sense out of them.

Humor is essential to a successful tactician, for the most potent weapons known to mankind are satire and ridicule.

A sense of humor enables him to maintain his perspective and see himself for what he really is: a bit of dust that burns for a fleeting second. A sense of humor is incompatible with the complete acceptance of any dogma, any religious, political, or economic prescription for salvation. It synthesizes with curiosity, irreverence, and imagination. The organizer has a personal identity of his own that cannot be lost by absorption or acceptance of any kind of group discipline or organization. I now begin to understand what I stated somewhat intuitively in *Reveille for Radicals* almost twenty years ago, that "the organizer in order to be part of all can be part of none."

A bit of a blurred vision of a better world. Much of an organizer's daily work is detail, repetitive and deadly in its monotony. In the totality of things he is engaged in one small bit. It is as though as an artist he is painting a tiny leaf. It is inevitable that sooner or later he will react with "What am I doing spending my whole life just painting one little leaf? The hell with it, I quit." What keeps him going is a blurred vision of a great mural where other artists—organizers—are painting their bits, and each piece is essential to the total.

An organized personality. The organizer must be well organized himself so he can be comfortable in a disorganized situation, rational in a sea of irrationalities. It is vital that he be able to accept and work with irrationalities for the purpose of change.

With very rare exceptions, the right things are done for the wrong reasons. It is futile to demand that men do the right thing for the right reason—this is a fight with a windmill. The organizer should know and accept that the right reason is only introduced as a moral rationalization after the right end has been achieved, although it may have been achieved for the wrong reason—therefore he should search for and use the wrong reasons to achieve the right goals. He should be able, with skill and calculation, to use irrationality in his attempts to progress toward a rational world.

For a variety of reasons the organizer must develop multiple issues. First, a wide-based membership can only be built on many issues. When we were building our organization in the Back of the Yards, the Polish Roman Catholic churches in Chicago joined us because they were concerned about the expanding power of the Irish Roman Catholic churches. The Packing House Workers Union was with us—so their rival unions joined, trying to counteract the potential membership and power pickup. We didn't, of course, care why they'd joined us—we just knew we'd be better off if they did.

The organizer recognizes that each person or bloc has a hierarchy of values. For instance, let us assume that we are in a ghetto community where everyone is for civil rights.

A black man there had bought a small house when the neighborhood was first changing, and he wound up paying a highly inflated price—more than four times the value of the property. Everything he owns is tied into that house. Urban renewal, now, is threatening to come in and take it on the basis of a value appraisal according to their criteria, which would be less than a fourth of his financial commitment. He is desperately trying to save his own small economic world. Civil rights would get him to a meeting once a month, maybe he'd sign some petitions and maybe he'd give a dollar here and there, but on a fight against urban renewal's threat to wipe out his property, he would come to meetings every night.

Next door to him is a woman who is renting. She is not concerned about urban renewal. She has three small girls, and her major worry is the drug pushers and pimps that infest the neighborhood and threaten the future of her children. She is for civil rights too, but she is more concerned about a community free of pimps and pushers; and she wants better schools for her children. Those are her No. 1 priorities.

Next door to her is a family on welfare; their No. 1 priority is more money. Across the street there is a family who can be described as the working poor, struggling to get along on their drastically limited budget—to them, consumer prices and local merchants' gouging are the No. 1 priorities. Any tenant of a slum landlord, living among rats and cockroaches, will quickly tell you what his No. 1 priority is—and so it goes. In a multiple-issue organization, each person is saying to the other, "I can't get what I want alone and neither can you. Let's make a deal: I'll support you for what you want and you support me for what I want." Those deals become the program.

Not only does a single- or even a dual-issue organization condemn you to a small organization, it is axiomatic that a single-issue organization won't last. An organization needs action as an individual needs oxygen. With only one or two issues there will certainly be a lapse of action, and then comes death. Multiple issues mean constant action and life.

An organizer must become sensitive to everything that is happening around him. He is always learning, and every incident teaches him something. He notices that when a bus has only a few empty seats, the crowd trying to get on will push and shove; if there are many empty seats the crowd will be courteous and considerate; and he muses that in a world of opportunities for all there would be a change in human behavior for the good. In his constant examination of life and of himself he finds himself becoming more and more of an organized personality.

A well-integrated political schizoid. The organizer must become schizoid, politically, in order not to slip into becoming a true believer. Before men can act an issue must be polarized. Men will act when they are convinced that their cause is 100 per cent on the side of the angels and that the opposition are 100 per cent on the side of the devil. He knows that there can be no action until issues are polarized to this degree. I have already discussed an example in the Declaration of Independence—the Bill of Particulars that conspicuously omitted all the advantages the colonies had gained from the British and cited only the disadvantages.

What I am saying is that the organizer must be able to split himself into two parts—one part in the arena of action where he polarizes the issue to 100 to nothing, and helps to lead his forces into conflict, while the other part knows that when the time comes for negotiations that it really is only a 10 per cent difference—and yet both parts have to live comfortably with each other. Only a well-organized person can split and yet stay together. But this is what the organizer must do.

Ego. Throughout these desired qualities is interwoven a strong ego, one we might describe as monumental in terms of solidity. Here we are using the word *ego* as discussed in the previous chapter, clearly differentiated from egotism. Ego is unreserved confidence in one's ability to do what he believes must be done. An organizer must accept, without fear or worry, that the odds are always against him. Having this kind of ego, he is a doer and does. The thought of copping out never stays with him for more than a fleeting moment; life is action.

A free and open mind, and political relativity. The organizer in his way of life, with his curiosity, irreverence, imagination, sense of humor, distrust of dogma, his self-organization, his understanding of the irrationality of much of human behavior, becomes a flexible personality, not a rigid structure that breaks when something unexpected happens. Having his own identity, he has no need for the security of an ideology or a panacea. He knows that life is a quest for uncertainty; that the only certain fact of life is uncertainty; and he can live with it. He knows that all values are relative, in a world of political relativity. Because of these qualities he is unlikely to disintegrate into cynicism and disillusionment, for he does not depend on illusion.

Finally, the organizer is constantly creating the new out of the old. He knows that all new ideas arise from conflict; that every time man has had a new idea it has been a challenge to the sacred ideas of the past and the present and inevitably a conflict has raged. Curiosity, irreverence, imagination, sense of humor, a free and open mind, an acceptance of the relativity of values and of the uncertainty of life, all inevitably fuse into the kind of person whose greatest joy is creation. He conceives of creation as the very essence of the meaning of life. In his constant striving for the new, he finds that he cannot endure what is repetitive and unchanging. For him hell would be doing the same thing over and over again.

This is the basic difference between the leader and the organizer. The leader goes on to build power to fulfill his desires, to hold and wield the power for purposes both social and personal. He wants power himself. The organizer finds his goal in creation of power for others to use.

These qualities are present in any free, creative person, whether an educator, or in the arts, or in any part of life. In "Adam Smith's" *The Money Game,* the characteristics of the desirable fund manager are described:

> It is personal intuition, sensing patterns of behavior. There is always something unknown, undiscerned. . . . You can't just graduate an analyst into managing funds. What is it the good managers have? It's a kind of locked-in concentration, an intuition, a feel, nothing that can be schooled. The first thing you have to know is yourself. A man who knows himself can step outside himself and watch his own reactions like an observer.

One would think that this was a description of an organizer but in everything creative, whether it is organizing a mutual fund or a mutual society, one is on the hunt for these qualities. Why one becomes an organizer instead of something else is, I suspect, due to a difference of degree of intensity of specific elements or relationships between them—or accident.

Communication

ONE CAN LACK any of the qualities of an organizer—with one exception—and still be effective and successful. That exception is the art of communication. It does not matter what you know about anything if you cannot communicate to your people. In that event you are not even a failure. You're just not there.

Communication with others takes place when they understand what you're trying to get across to them. If they don't understand, then you are not communicating regardless of words, pictures, or anything else. People only understand things in terms of their experience, which means that you must get within their experience. Further, communication is a two-way process. If you try to get your ideas across to others without paying attention to what they have to say to you, you can forget about the whole thing.

I know that I have communicated with the other party when his eyes light up and he responds, "I know exactly what you mean. I had something just like that happen to me once. Let me tell you about it!" Then I know that there has been communication. Recently I flew from

O'Hare Airport in Chicago to New York. After the jet pulled away from the gate we heard the familiar announcement, "This is your captain speaking. I am sorry to advise you that we are No. 18 for take-off. I am turning off the 'No Smoking' sign and will keep you posted."

Many a captain feels compelled to keep you "entertained" with an incessant stream of verbal garbage. "You will be interested to know that this airplane fully loaded weighs blah blah tons." You couldn't care less. Or, "Our flight plan will carry us over Bazickus, Ohio, and then Junkspot," etc., etc. However, on this trip the captain of the plane touched on the experience of many of the passengers and really communicated. In the midst of his "entertainment" he commented: "Incidentally, I will let you know when we get the take-off clearance and from the instant you hear those jets roar for the take-off until the instant of lift-off, we will have consumed enough fuel for you to drive an automobile from Chicago to New York and back with detours as well!" You could hear such comments as, "Oh, come on—he must be kidding." With the announcement of clearance and the take-off run, passengers all over the plane were looking at their watches. At the end of approximately 25 seconds to lift-off passengers were turning to each other saying, "Would you believe it?" It was evident that, as you might expect, many passengers had been concerned at some time with the number of miles a car could travel on a given amount of gas.

Educators are in common agreement on this concept of communication, even though few teachers use it. But after all, there are only a few real teachers in that profession.

An educational leader makes this point of understanding and experience in a very personal way:

"When he has had experience of life." Read
Homer and Horace by all means, says Newman;
feed mind and eye and ear with their images and
language and music; but do not expect to understand what they are really talking about before
you are forty.

This truth was first brought home to me
more than thirty years ago one December day,
as I walked down the road from Argentieres to
Chamonix after a snowfall, and suddenly from
the abyss of unconscious memory a line of Virgil
rose into my mind and I found myself repeating
  Sed iacet aggeribus niveis informis et alto
  Terra gelu.
I had read the words at school and no doubt
translated them glibly "the earth lies formless
under snow-drifts and deep frost"; but suddenly,
with the snow scene before my eyes, I perceived
for the first time what Virgil meant by the epithet
informis, "without form," and how perfectly it
describes the work of snow, which literally does
make the world formless, blurring the sharp out-
lines of roofs and eaves, of pines and rocks and
mountain ridges, taking from them their definite-
ness of shape and form. Yet how many times
before that day had I read the words without
seeing what they really mean! It is not that the
word *informis* meant nothing to me when I was
an undergraduate; but it meant much less than
its full meaning. Personal experience was necessary to real understanding.

—Sir Richard Livingstone, *On Education*, New
York, 1945, p. 13.

Every now and then I have been accused of being
crude and vulgar because I have used analogies of sex or
the toilet. I do not do this because I want to shock,

particularly, but because there are certain experiences common to all, and sex and toilet are two of them. Furthermore, everyone is interested in those two—which can't be said of every common experience. I remember explaining relativity in morals by telling the following story. A question is put to three women, one American, one British, and one French: What would they do if they found themselves shipwrecked on a desert island with six sex-hungry men? The American woman said she would try to hide and build a raft at night or send up smoke signals in order to escape. The British woman said she would pick the strongest man and shack up with him, so that he could protect her from the others. The French woman looked up quizzically and asked, "What's the problem?"

Since people understand only in terms of their own experience, an organizer must have at least a cursory familiarity with their experience. It not only serves communication but it strengthens the personal identification of the organizer with the others, and facilitates further communication. For example, in one community there was a Greek Orthodox priest, who will be called here the Archimandrite Anastopolis. Every Saturday night, faithfully followed by six of his church members, he would tour the local taverns. After some hours of imbibing he would suddenly stiffen, and become so drunk that he was paralyzed. At this point his faithful six, like pallbearers, would carry him through the streets back to the safety of his church. Over the years it became part of the community's experience, in fact a living legend. In talking to anyone in that neighborhood you could not communicate the fact that something was out of place, not with it, except to say it was "out like the Archimandrite." The response would be laughter, nodding of heads, a "Yeah, we know what you mean"—but also an intimacy of sharing a common experience.

When you are trying to communicate and can't find the point in the experience of the other party at which he can receive and understand, then, you must create the experience for him.

I was trying to explain to two staff organizers in training how their problems in their community arose because they had gone outside the experience of their people: that when you go outside anyone's experience not only do you not communicate, you cause confusion. They had earnest, intelligent expressions on their faces and were verbally and visually agreeing and understanding, but I knew they really didn't understand and that I was not communicating. I had not got into their experience. So I had to give them an experience. -

We were having lunch in a restaurant at the time. I called their attention to the luncheon menu listing eight items or combinations and all numbered. Item No. 1 was bacon and eggs, potatoes, toast and coffee; Item No. 2, something else, and Item No. 6 was a chicken-liver omelet. I explained that the waiter was conditioned in terms of his experience to immediately translate any order into its accompanying number. He would listen to the words "bacon and eggs," etc. but his mind had already clicked "No. 1." The only variation was whether the eggs were to be done easy or the bacon very crisp, in which case he would call out, "No. 1, easy," or a variation thereof.

With this clear, I said, "Now, when the waiter takes my order, instead of my saying 'a chicken-liver omelet,' which to him is No. 6, I will go outside his area of experience and say 'You see this chicken-liver omelet?' He will respond, 'Yes, No. 6.' I will say, 'Well, just a minute. I don't want the chicken livers in the omelet. I want the omelet with the chicken livers on the side—now, is that clear?' He will say it is, and then the odds are 9 to 1 everything is going to get screwed up because he can't just order No. 6 any more. I don't know what will happen but I have gone outside his accepted area of experience."

The waiter took my order precisely as I have described above. In about twenty minutes he returned with an omelet and a full order of chicken livers, as well as a bill for $3.25—$1.75 for the omelet and $1.50 for the chicken livers. I objected and immediately took issue, pointing out that all I had wanted was No. 6, the total price of which was $1.50, but that instead of having the livers mixed in with the omelet, I had wanted them on the side. Now there was a full omelet, a full order of chicken livers, and a bill for nearly three times the menu price. Furthermore I could not eat a full order of chicken livers as well as the omelet. Confusion came down. Waiter and manager huddled. Finally the waiter returned, flushed and upset: "Sorry about the mistake—everybody got mixed up —eat whatever you want." The bill was changed back to the original price for No. 6.

In a similar situation in Los Angeles four staff members and I were talking in front of the Biltmore Hotel when I demonstrated the same point, saying: "Look, I am holding a ten-dollar bill in my hand. I propose to walk around the Biltmore Hotel, a total of four blocks, and try to give it away. This will certainly be outside of everyone's experience. You four walk behind me and watch the faces of the people I'll approach. I am going to go up to them holding out this ten-dollar bill and say, 'Here, take this.' My guess is that everyone will back off, look confused, insulted, or fearful, and want to get away from this nut fast.

From their experience when someone approaches them he is either out to ask for instructions or to panhandle— particularly the way I'm dressed, no coat or tie."

I walked around, trying to give the ten-dollar bill away. The reactions were all "within the experiences of the people." About three of them, seeing the ten-dollar bill, spoke first—"I'm sorry. I don't have any change." Others hurried past saying, "I'm sorry, I don't have any money on me right now," as though I had been trying to get money from them instead of trying to give them money. One young woman flared up, almost screaming, "I'm not that kind of a girl and if you don't get away from here, I'll call a cop!" Another woman in her thirties snarled, "I don't come that cheap!" There was one man who stopped and said, "What kind of a con game is this?" and then walked away. Most of the people responded with shock, confusion, and silence, and they quickened their pace and sort of walked around me.

After approximately fourteen people, I found myself back at the front entrance of the Biltmore Hotel, still holding my ten-dollar bill. My four companions had, then, a clearer understanding of the concept that people react strictly on the basis of their own experience.

For another example of the same principle, here is a Christian civilization where most people have gone to church and have mouthed various Christian doctrines, and yet this is really not part of their experience because they haven't lived it. Their church experience has been purely a ritualistic decoration.

The *New York Times* some years ago reported the case of a man who converted to Catholicism at around the age of forty and then, filled with the zeal of a convert, determined to emulate as far as possible the life of St. Francis of Assisi. He withdrew his life's savings, about $2,300. He took this money out in $5 bills. Armed with his bundle of $5 bills, he went down to the poorest section of New York City, the Bowery (this was before the time of urban renewal), and every time a needy-looking man or woman passed by him he would step up and say, "Please take this." Now, the difference between this situation and mine around the Biltmore Hotel is that the panhandlers on the Bowery would not find an offer of money or of a bowl of soup outside their experience. At any rate, our friend attempting to live a Christian life and emulate St. Francis of Assisi found that he could do so for only forty minutes before being arrested by a Christian police officer, driven to Bellevue Hospital by a Christian ambulance doctor, and pronounced non compos mentis by a Christian psychiatrist. Christianity is beyond the experience of a Christian-professing-but-not-practicing population.

In mass organization, you can't go outside of people's actual experience. I've been asked, for example, why I never talk to a Catholic priest or a Protestant minister or a rabbi in terms of the Judaeo-Christian ethic or the Ten Commandments or the Sermon on the Mount. I never talk in those terms. Instead I approach them on the basis of their own self-interest, the welfare of their Church, even its physical property.

If I approached them in a moralistic way, it would be outside their experience, because Christianity and Judaeo-Christianity are outside of the experience of organized religion. They would just listen to me and very sympathetically tell me how noble I was. And the moment I walked out they'd call their secretaries in and say, "If that screwball ever shows up again, tell him I'm out."

Communication for persuasion, as in negotiation, is

more than entering the area of another person's experience.
It is getting a fix on his main value or goal and holding
your course on that target. You don't communicate with
anyone purely on the rational facts or ethics of an issue.
The spisode between Moses and God, when the Jews had
begun to worship the Golden Calf,° is revealing. Moses did
not try to communicate with God in terms of mercy or
justice when God was angry and wanted to destroy the
Jews; he moved in on a top value and outmaneuvered God.
It is only when the other party is concerned or feels
threatened that he will listen—in the arena of action, a
threat or a crisis becomes almost a precondition to communication.

A great organizer, like Moses, never loses his cool as
a lesser man might have done when God said: "Go, get

° "And the Lord spoke to Moses, saying: Go, get thee down: thy people,
which thou hast brought out of the land of Egypt hath sinned.

"They have quickly strayed from the way which thou didst shew
them: and they have made to themselves a molten calf and have adored
it, and sacrificing victims to it, have said: These are thy gods, O Israel,
that have brought thee out of the land of Egypt.

"And again the Lord said to Moses: See that this people is stiff
necked:

"Let me alone, that my wrath may be kindled against them, and that
I may destroy them, and I will make of thee a great nation.

"But Moses besought the Lord his God, saying: Why, O Lord, is thy
indignation enkindled against thy people, whom thou hast brought out of
the land of Egypt, with great power, and with a mighty hand?

"Let not the Egyptians say, I beseech thee: He craftily brought them
out that he might kill them in the mountains, and destroy them from the
earth: let thy anger cease, and be appeased upon the wickedness of
thy people.

"Remember Abraham, Isaac, and Israel, thy servants, to whom thou
sworest by thy own self, saying: I will multiply your seed as the stars
of heaven: and this whole land that I have spoken of, I will give to your
seed, and you shall possess it for ever.

"And the Lord was appeased from doing the evil which he had
spoken against his people."

—Exodus 32: 7-14, Douay-Rheims ed.

thee down: *thy* people, whom *thou* hast brought out of the land of Egypt hath sinned." At that point, if Moses had dropped his cool in any way, one would have expected him to reply, "Where do you get off with all that stuff about *my* people whom *I* brought out of the land of Egypt . . . I was just taking a walk through the desert and who started that bush burning, and who told me to get over to Egypt, and who told me to get those people out of slavery, and who pulled all the power plays, and all the plagues, and who split the Red Sea, and who put a pillar of clouds up in the sky, and now all of a sudden they become *my* people."

But Moses kept his cool, and he knew that the most important center of his attack would have to be on what he judged to be God's prime value. As Moses read it, it was that God wanted to be No. 1. All through the Old Testament one bumps into "there shall be no other Gods before me," "Thou shalt not worship false gods," "I am a jealous and vindictive God," "Thou shalt not use the Lord's name in vain." And so it goes, on and on, including the first part of the Ten Commandments.

Knowing this, Moses took off on his attack. He began arguing and telling God to cool it. (At this point, trying to figure out Moses' motivations, one would wonder whether it was because he was loyal to his own people, or felt sorry for them, or whether he just didn't want the job of breeding a whole new people, because after all he was pushing 120 and that's asking a lot.) At any rate, he began to negotiate, saying, "Look, God, you're God. You're holding all the cards. Whatever you want to do you can do and nobody can stop you. But you know, God, you just can't scratch that deal you've got with these people—you remember, the Covenant—in which you promised them not only to take them out of slavery but that they would practically inherit the earth. Yeah, I know, you're going to tell me that they broke their end of it all so all bets are off. But it isn't that easy. You're in a spot. The news of this deal has leaked out all over the joint. The Egyptians, Philistines, Canaanites, *everybody* knows about it. But, as I said before, you're God. Go ahead and knock them off. What do you care if people are going to say, 'There goes God. You can't believe anything he tells you. You can't make a deal with him. His word isn't even worth the stone it's written on.' But after all, you're God and I suppose you can handle it."

And the Lord was appeased from doing the evil which he had spoken against his people.

Another maxim in effective communication is that people have to make their own decisions. It isn't just that Moses couldn't tell God what God should do; no organizer can tell a community, either, what to do. Much of the time, though, the organizer will have a pretty good idea of what the community should be doing, and he will want to suggest, maneuver, and persuade the community toward that action. He will not ever seem to tell the community what to do; instead, he will use loaded questions. For example, in a meeting on tactics where the organizer is convinced that tactic Z is the thing to do:

ORGANIZER: What do you think we should do now?
COMMUNITY LEADER No. 1: I think we should do tactic X.
ORGANIZER: What do you think, Leader No. 2?
LEADER No. 2: Yeah, that sounds pretty good to me.
ORGANIZER: What about you, No. 3?

LEADER No. 3: Well, I don't know. It sounds good but something worries me. What do you think, organizer?

ORGANIZER: The important thing is what you guys think. What's the something that worries you?

LEADER No. 3: I don't know—it's something—

ORGANIZER: I got a hunch that—I don't know, but I remember yesterday you and No. 1 talking and explaining to me something about somebody who once tried something like tactic X and it left him wide open because of this and that so it didn't work or something. Remember telling me about that, No. 1?

LEADER No. 1 (who has been listening and now knows tactic X won't work): Sure. Sure. I remember. Yeah, well, we all know X won't work.

ORGANIZER: Yeah. We also know that unless we put out all the things that won't work, we'll never get to the one that will. Right?

LEADER No. 1 (fervently): Absolutely!

And so the guided questioning goes on without anyone losing face or being left out of the decision-making. Every weakness of every proposed tactic is probed by questions. Eventually someone suggests tactic Z, and, again through questions, its positive features emerge and it is decided on.

Is this manipulation? Certainly, just as a teacher manipulates, and no less, even a Socrates. As time goes on and education proceeds, the leadership becomes increasingly sophisticated. The organizer recedes from the local circle of decision-makers. His response to questions about what *he* thinks becomes a non-directive counterquestion, "What do you think?" His job becomes one of weaning the group away from any dependency upon him. Then his job is done.

While the organizer proceeds on the basis of questions, the community leaders always regard his judgment above their own. They believe that he knows his job, he knows the right tactics, that's why he is their organizer. The organizer knows that even if they feel that way consciously, if he starts issuing orders and "explaining," it would begin to build up a subconscious resentment, a feeling that the organizer is putting them down, is not respecting their dignity as individuals. The organizer knows that it is a human characteristic that someone who asks for help and gets it reacts not only with gratitude but with a subconscious hostility toward the one who helped him. It is a sort of psychic "original sin" because he feels that the one who helped him is always aware that if it hadn't been for his help, he would still be a defeated nothing. All this involves a skillful and sensitive role-playing on the part of the organizer. In the beginning the organizer is the general, he knows where, what, and how, but he never wears his four stars, never is addressed as nor acts as a general—he is an organizer.

There are times, too—plenty of them—when the organizer discovers in the course of discussions like the one above that tactic Z, or whatever it was he decided on ahead of time, is not the appropriate tactic. At this point, let's hope his ego is strong enough to allow someone else to have the answer.

One of the factors that changes what you can and can't communicate is relationships. There are sensitive areas that one does not touch until there is a strong personal relationship based on common involvements. Otherwise the other party turns off and literally does not hear, regardless of whether your words are within his experience.

Conversely, if you have a good relationship, he is very receptive, and your "message" comes through in a positive context.

For example, I have always believed that birth control and abortion are personal rights to be exercised by the individual. If, in my early days when I organized the Back of the Yards neighborhood in Chicago, which was 95 per cent Roman Catholic, I had tried to communicate this, even through the experience of the residents, whose economic plight was aggravated by large families, that would have been the end of my relationship with the community. That instant I would have been stamped as an enemy of the church and all communication would have ceased. Some years later, after establishing solid relationships, I was free to talk about anything, including birth control. I remember discussing it with the then Catholic Chancellor. By then the argument was no longer limited to such questions as, "How much longer do you think the Catholic Church can hang on to this archaic notion and still survive?" I remember seeing five priests in the waiting room who wanted to see the chancellor, and knowing his contempt for each one of them, I said, "Look, I'll prove to you that you do really believe in birth control even though you are making all kinds of noises against it," and then I opened the door, saying, "Take a look out there. Can you look at them and tell me you oppose birth control?" He cracked up and said "That's an unfair argument and you know it," but the subject and nature of the discussion would have been unthinkable without that solid relationship.

A classic example of the failure to communicate because the organizer has gone completely outside the experience of the people, is the attempt by campus activists to indicate to the poor the bankruptcy of their prevailing values. "Take my word for it—if you get a good job and a split-level ranch house out in the suburbs, a color TV, two cars, and money in the bank, that just won't bring you happiness." The response without exception is always, "Yeah. Let me be the judge of that one—I'll let you know after I get it."

Communication on a general basis without being fractured into the specifics of experience becomes rhetoric and it carries a very limited meaning. It is the difference between being informed of the death of a quarter of a million people—which becomes a statistic—or the death of one or two close friends or loved ones or members of one's family. In the latter it becomes the full emotional impact of the finality of tragedy. In trying to explain what the personal relationship means, I have told various audiences, "If the chairman of this meeting had opened up by saying, 'I am shocked and sorry to have to report to you that we have just been notified that Mr. Alinsky has just been killed in a plane crash and therefore this lecture is canceled,' the only reaction you would have would be, 'Well, gee, that's too bad. I wonder what he was like, but oh, well, let's see, what are we going to do this evening. We've got the evening free now. We could go to a movie.' And that is all that one would expect, except of those who have known me in the past, regardless of what the relationship was.

"Now suppose after finishing this lecture, let us assume that all of you have disagreed with everything I have said; you don't like my face, the sound of my voice, my manner, my clothes, you just don't like me, period. Let us further assume that I am to lecture to you again next week, and at that time you are informed of my sudden death. Your reaction will be very different, regardless of your dislike. You will react with shock: you will say, 'Why, just yesterday he was alive, breathing, talking, and laughing. It just seems incredible to believe that suddenly like that he's gone.' This is the human reaction to a personal relationship."

What is of particular importance here however is the fact that you were dealing with one specific person and not a general mass.

It is what was implicit in the reputed statement of that organizational genius Samuel Adams, at the time when he was allegedly planning the Boston Massacre; he was quoted as saying that there ought to be no less than three or four killed so that we will have martyrs for the Revolution, but there must be no more than ten, because after you get beyond that number we no longer have martyrs but simply a sewage problem.

This is the problem in trying to communicate on the issue of the H bomb. It is too big. It involves too many casualties. It is beyond the experience of people and they just react with, "Yeah, it is a terrible thing," but it really does not grip them. It is the same thing with figures. The moment one gets into the area of $25 million and above, let alone a billion, the listener is completely out of touch, no longer really interested, because the figures have gone above his experience and almost are meaningless. Millions of Americans do not know how many million dollars make up a billion.

This element of the specific that must be small enough to be grasped by the hands of experience ties very definitely into the whole scene of *issues*. Issues must be able to be communicated. It is essential that they can be communicated. It is essential that they be simple enough to be grasped as rallying or battle cries. They cannot be generalities like sin or immorality or the good life or morals. They must be *this* immorality of *this* slum landlord with *this* slum tenement where *these* people suffer.

It should be obvious by now that communication occurs concretely, by means of one's specific experience. General theories become meaningful only when one has absorbed and understood the specific constituents and then related them back to a general concept. Unless this is done, the specifics become nothing more than a string of interesting anecdotes. That is the world as it is in communication.

In the
Beginning

IN THE BEGINNING the incoming organizer must establish his identity or, putting it another way, get his license to operate. He must have a reason for being there —a reason acceptable to the people.

Any stranger is suspect. "Who's the cat?" "What's he asking all those questions for?" "Is he really the cops or the F.B.I.?" "What's his bag?" "What's he really after?" "What's in it for him?" "Who's he working for?"

The answers to these questions must be acceptable in terms of the experience of the community. If the organizer begins with an affirmation of his love for people, he promptly turns everyone off. If, on the other hand, he begins with a denunciation of exploiting employers, slum landlords, police shakedowns, gouging merchants, he is inside their experience and they accept him. People can make judgments only on the basis of their own experiences. And the question in their minds is, "If we were in the organizer's position, would we do what he is doing and if so, why?" Until they have an answer that is at least somewhat acceptable they find it difficult to understand and accept the organizer.

His acceptance as an organizer depends on his success in convincing key people—and many others—first, that he is on their side, and second, that he has ideas, and knows how to fight to change things; that he's not one of these guys "doing his thing," that he's a winner. Otherwise who needs him? All his presence means is that the census changes from 225,000 to 225,001.

It is not enough to persuade them of your competence, talents, and courage—they must have faith in your ability and courage. They must believe in your capacity not just to provide the opportunity for action, power, change, adventure, a piece of the drama of life, but to give a very definite promise, almost an assurance of victory. They must also have faith in your courage to fight the oppressive establishment—courage that they, too, will begin to get once they have the protective armor of a power organization, but don't have during the first lonely steps forward.

Love and faith are not common companions. More commonly power and fear consort with faith. The Have-Nots have a limited faith in the worth of their own judgments. They still look to the judgments of the Haves. They respect the strength of the upper class and they believe that the Haves are more intelligent, more competent, and endowed with "something special." Distance has a way of enhancing power, so that respect becomes tinged with reverence. The Haves are the authorities and thus the beneficiaries of the various myths and legends that always develop around power. The Have-Nots will believe them where they would be hesitant and uncertain about their own judgments. Power is not to be crossed; one must respect and obey. Power means strength, whereas love is a human frailty the people mistrust. It is a sad fact of life that power and fear are the fountainheads of faith.

The job of the organizer is to maneuver and bait the establishment so that it will publicly attack him as a "dangerous enemy." The word "enemy" is sufficient to put the organizer on the side of the people, to identify him with the Have-Nots, but it is not enough to endow him with the special qualities that induce fear and thus give him the means to establish his own power against the establishment. Here again we find that it is power and fear that are essential to the development of faith. This need is met by the establishment's use of the brand "dangerous," for in that one word the establishment reveals its fear of the organizer, its fear that he represents a threat to its omnipotence. Now the organizer has his "birth certificate" and can begin.

In 1939, when I first began to organize back of the old Chicago stockyards, on the site of Upton Sinclair's *Jungle,* I acted in such a way that within a few weeks the meatpackers publicly pronounced me a "subversive menace." The *Chicago Tribune*'s adoption of me as a public enemy of law and order, "a radical's radical," gave me a perennial and constantly renewable baptismal certificate in the city of Chicago. A generation later, in a black community on Chicago's South Side, next to my alma mater, the University of Chicago, it was the university's virulent personal attack on me, augmented by attacks by the press, that strengthened my credentials with a black community somewhat suspicious of white skin. Eastman Kodak and the Gannett newspaper chain did the same for me in Rochester, New York. In both black ghettos, in Chicago and in Rochester, the reaction was: "The way the fat-cat white newspapers are ripping hell out of Alinsky—he must be all right!" I could very easily have gone into either Houston, Texas or Oakland, California; in the former, the

Ku Klux Klan appeared at the airport in full regalia, with threats against my personal security. The Houston press printed charges against me by the Mayor of Houston, and there was a mass picket line by the John Birch Society. In Oakland, the City Council, fearing the possibility of my coming into Oakland, passed a widely publicized special resolution declaring me unwelcome in the city. In both cases, the black communities were treated to the spectacle of seeing the establishment react with unusually severe fear and hysteria.

Establishing one's credentials of competency is only part of the organizer's first job. He needs other credentials to begin—credentials that enable him to meet the question, "Who asked you to come in here?" with the answer, "You did." He must be invited by a significant sector of the local population, their churches, street organizations, social clubs, or other groups.

Today my notoriety and the hysterical instant reaction of the establishment not only validate my credentials of competency but also ensure automatic popular invitation. An example was the invitation into the black ghettos in Rochester.

In 1964 Rochester exploded in a bloody race riot resulting in the calling of the National Guard, the fatal crash of a police helicopter, and considerable loss of life and property. In its wake, the city was numb with shock. A city proud of its affluence, culture, and progressive churches, was dazed and guilt-ridden at its rude discovery of the misery of life in the ghetto and of its failure to do anything about it. The City Council of Churches, representing the Protestant churches, approached me and asked me if I would be available to help organize the black ghetto to get equality, jobs, housing, quality education, and particularly power to participate in the decision-making in all public programs involving their people. They also demanded that the representatives of the black community be those chosen by the blacks and not those selected by the white establishment. I advised the church council of the cost and said that my organization was available. The council agreed to the cost and "invited" us to come in and organize. I replied, then, that the churches had a right to invite us in to organize *their* people in *their* neighborhoods, but that they had no right to speak for, let alone invite anyone into, the black community. I emphasized that we were not a colonial power like the churches who sent their missionaries everywhere whether they were invited or not. The black community had been silent—but at that point panic gripped the white establishment. The Rochester press, in front page stories and editorials, raised the cry that if I came to Rochester it would mean the end of good fellowship, of Brotherhood Week, of Christian understanding between black and white! It meant that I would say to the blacks, "The only way you can get your legitimate rights is to organize, get the power and tell the white establishment 'either come around or else!'" The blacks read and heard and agreed. Between the press and the mass media you would have assumed that my coming to Rochester was equivalent to the city's being invaded by the Russians, the Chinese, and the bubonic plague. Rochesterians will never forget it, and one had to be there to believe it. And so we were invited in by nearly every church and organization in the ghetto and by petitions signed by thousands of ghetto residents. Now we had a legitimate right to be there, even more of a right than any of the inviting organizations in the ghetto, for even they had not been invited in by the mass of their community.

This advantage is the dividend of reputation, but the important issue here is how the organizer without a reputation gets the invitation.

The organizer's job is to inseminate an invitation for himself, to agitate, introduce ideas, get people pregnant with hope and a desire for change and to identify you as the person most qualified for this purpose. Here the tool of the organizer, in the agitation leading to the invitation as well as actual organization and education of local leadership, is the use of the question, the Socratic method:

ORGANIZER: Do you live over in that slummy building?

ANSWER: Yeah. What about it?

ORGANIZER: What the hell do you live there for?

ANSWER: What do you mean, what do I live there for? Where else am I going to live? I'm on welfare.

ORGANIZER: Oh, you mean you pay rent in that place?

ANSWER: Come on, is this a put-on? Very funny! You know where you can live for free?

ORGANIZER: Hmm. That place looks like it's crawling with rats and bugs.

ANSWER: It sure is.

ORGANIZER: Did you ever try to get that landlord to do anything about it?

ANSWER: Try to get him to do anything about anything! If you don't like it, get out. That's all he has to say. There are plenty more waiting.

ORGANIZER: What if you didn't pay your rent?

ANSWER: They'd throw us out in ten minutes.

ORGANIZER: Hmm. What if nobody in that building paid their rent?

ANSWER: Well, they'd start to throw . . . Hey, you know, they'd have trouble throwing everybody out, wouldn't they?

ORGANIZER: Yeah, I guess they would.

ANSWER: Hey, you know, maybe you got something—say, I'd like you to meet some of my friends. How about a drink?

POLICY AFTER POWER

One of the great problems in the beginning of an organization is, often, that the people do not know what they want. Discovering this stirs up, in the organizer, that inner doubt shared by so many, whether the masses of people are competent to make decisions for a democratic society. It is the schizophrenia of a free society that we outwardly espouse faith in the people but inwardly have strong doubts whether the people can be trusted. These reservations can destroy the effectiveness of the most creative and talented organizer. Many times, contact with low-income groups does not fire one with enthusiasm for the political gospel of democracy. This disillusionment comes partly because we romanticize the poor in a way we romanticize other sectors of society, and partly because when you talk with any people you find yourselves confronted with clichés, a variety of superficial, stereotyped responses, and a general lack of information. In a black ghetto if you ask, "What's wrong?" you are told, "Well, the schools are segregated." "What do you think should be done to make better schools?" "Well, they should be desegregated." "How?" "Well, you know." And if you say you don't know, then a lack of knowledge or an inability on the part of the one you are talking to may show itself in a defensive, hostile reaction: "You whites were responsible for the segregation in the first place. We didn't do it. So it's your problem, not ours. You started it, you finish it." If you pursue the point by asking, "Well, what else is wrong with the schools right now?" you get the answer, "The buildings are old; the teachers are bad. We've got to have change." "Well, what kind of change?" "Well, everybody knows things have to be changed." That is usually the end of the line. If you push it any further, you come again to a hostile, defensive reaction or to withdrawal as they suddenly remember they have to be somewhere else.

The issue that is not clear to organizers, missionaries, educators, or any outsider, is simply that if people feel they don't have the power to change a bad situation, *then they do not think about it*. Why start figuring out how you are going to spend a million dollars if you do not have a million dollars or are ever going to have a million dollars —unless you want to engage in fantasy?

Once people are organized so that they have the power to make changes, then, when confronted with questions of change, they begin to think and to ask questions about how to make the changes. If the teachers in the schools are bad then what do we mean by a bad teacher? What is a good teacher? How do we get good teachers? When we say our children do not understand what the teachers are talking about and our teachers do not understand what the children are talking about, then we ask how communication can be established. *Why* cannot teachers communicate with the children and the latter with the teachers. What are the hangups? Why don't the teachers understand what the values are in our neighborhood? How can we make them understand? All these and many other perceptive questions begin to arise. It is when people have a genuine opportunity to act and to change conditions that they begin to think their problems through —then they show their competence, raise the right questions, seek special professional counsel and look for the answers. Then you begin to realize that believing in people is not just a romantic myth. But here you see that the first requirement for communication and education is for people to *have a reason* for knowing. It is the creation of the instrument or the circumstances of power that provides the reason and makes knowledge essential. Remember, too, that a powerless people will not be purposefully curious about life, and that they then cease being alive.

Something else that comes with experience is the knowledge that the resolution of a particular problem will bring on another problem. The organizer may know this, but he doesn't mention it; if he did he would invite, and encounter, a feeling of futility on the part of the others. "Why bother doing this if it means another problem? We fight and win and what have we won? So let's forget it."

He knows too that what we fight for now as matters of life and death will be soon forgotten, and changed situations will change desires and issues. It is common for policy to be the product of power. You begin to build power for a particular program—then the program changes when some power has been built. The reaction of the Woodlawn leaders was typical on this point.

In the beginning of the organization of the black ghetto of Woodlawn there were five major issues involving urban renewal, all centering on stopping the close-by University of Chicago from bulldozing the ghetto. The Woodlawn Organization quickly developed power and scored a series of victories. Eight months later the city of Chicago issued a new policy statement on urban renewal. That day the leaders of the Woodlawn Organization stormed into my office angrily denouncing the policy statement: "The city can't get away with this—who do they think they are? We'll put barricades in our streets—we'll fight!" Throughout the tirade it never occurred to any of the angry leaders that the city's new policy granted all the five demands for which the Woodlawn Organization began. Then they were fighting for hamburger; now they wanted filet mignon; so it goes. And why not?

An organizer knows that life is a sea of shifting desires, changing elements, of relativity and uncertainty, and yet he must stay within the experience of the people he is working with and act in terms of specific resolutions and answers, of definitiveness and certainty. To do otherwise would be to stifle organization and action, for what the organizer accepts as uncertainty would be seen by them as a terrifying chaos.

In the early days the organizer moves out front in any situation of risk where the power of the establishment can get someone's job, call in an overdue payment, or any other form of retaliation, partly because these dangers would cause many local people to back off from conflict. Here the organizer serves as a protective shield; if anything goes wrong it is all his fault, he has the responsibility. If they are successful all credit goes to the local people.

He acts as the septic tank in the early stages—he gets all the shit. Later, as power increases, the risks diminish, and gradually the people step out front to take the risks. This is part of the process of growing up, both for the local community leaders and for the organization.

The organizer must know and be sensitive to the shadows that surround him during his first days in the community. One of the shadows is that it is just about impossible for people to fully understand—much less adhere to—a totally new idea. The fear of change is, as discussed earlier, one of our deepest fears, and a new idea must be at the least couched in the language of past ideas; often, it must be, at first, diluted with vestiges of the past.

RATIONALIZATION

A large shadow over organizing efforts, in the beginning, is, then, rationalization. Everyone has a reason or rationalization for what he does or does not do. No matter what, every action carries its rationalization. One of Chicago's political ward bosses nationally notorious for his use of the chain ballot and multiple voting once unleashed a tirade well seasoned with alcohol on my being a disloyal American. He climaxed with, "And you, Alinsky! When that great day of America, election day, comes around— that day of the right to vote for which our ancestors fought and died—when that great day comes around you care so little for your country that you never even bother to vote more than once!"

Organizing, one must be aware of the tremendous importance of understanding the part played by rationalization on a mass basis—it is similar to the function on an individual basis. On a mass basis it is the community residents' and leadership's justification for why they have not been able to do anything until the organizer appeared. It is primarily a subconscious feeling that the organizer is looking down on them, wondering why they did not have the intelligence, so to speak, and the insights, to realize that through organization and the securing of power they could have resolved many of the problems they've lived with for these many years—why did they have to wait for him? With this going on in their minds they throw up a whole series of arguments against various organizational procedures, but they are not real arguments, simply attempts to justify the fact that they have not moved or organized in the past. Most people find this necessary, not only to justify themselves to the organizer, but also to themselves.

In an individual a psychiatrist would call these "rationalizations," as we call them here, "defenses." The patient has a series of defenses, which in therapy have to be broken through to get to the problem—which the patient then is compelled to confront. Chasing rationalizations is like attempting to find the rainbow. Rationalizations must be recognized as such so that the organizer does not get trapped in communication problems or in treating them as the real situations.

An extreme example, but one that very clearly spelled out the nature of rationalizations, came about three years ago when I met with various Canadian Indian leaders in the north of a Canadian province. I was there at the invitation of these leaders, who wanted to discuss their problems and solicit my advice. The problems of the Canadian Indians are very similar to those of the American Indians. They are on reservations, they are segregated, relatively speaking, and they suffer from all the general discriminatory practices Indians have been subjected to since the white man took over North America. In Canada the census figures on the Indian population range from 150,000 to 225,000 out of a total population estimated at between 22 and 24 million.

The conversation began with my suggesting that the general approach should be that the Indians get together, crossing all tribal lines, and organize. Because of their relatively small numbers I thought that they should then work with various sectors of the white liberal population, gain them as allies, and then begin to move nationally. Immediately I ran into the rationalizations. The dialogue went something like this (I should preface this by noting that it was quite obvious what was happening since I could see from the way the Indians were looking at each other they were thinking: "So we invite this white organizer from south of the border to come up here and he tells us to get organized and to do these things. What must be going through his mind is: 'What's wrong with you Indians that you have been sitting around here for a couple of hundred years now and you haven't organized to do these things?'" And so it began):

INDIANS: Well, we can't organize.
ME: Why not?
INDIANS: Because that's a white man's way of doing things.
ME (I decided to let that one pass though it obviously was untrue, since mankind from time immemorial has always organized, regardless of what race or color they

were, whenever they wanted to bring about change):
I don't understand.

INDIANS: Well, you see, if we organize, that means getting
out and fighting the way you are telling us to do and
that would mean that we would be corrupted by the
white man's culture and lose our own values.

ME: What are these values that you would lose?

INDIANS: Well, there are all kinds of values.

ME: Like what?

INDIANS: Well, there's creative fishing.

ME: What do you mean, creative fishing?

INDIANS: Creative fishing.

ME: I heard you the first time. What is this creative fishing?

INDIANS: Well, you see, when you whites go out and fish,
you just go out and fish, don't you?

ME: Yeah, I guess so.

INDIANS: Well, you see, when we go out and fish, we fish
creatively.

ME: Yeah. That's the third time you've come around with
that. What is this creative fishing?

INDIANS: Well, to begin with, when we go out fishing, we
get away from everything. We get way out in the woods.

ME: Well, we whites don't exactly go fishing in Times
Square, you know.

INDIANS: Yes, but it's different with us. When we go out,
we're out on the water and you can hear the lap of the
waves on the bottom of the canoe, and the birds in the
trees and the leaves rustling, and—you know what I
mean?

ME: No, I don't know what you mean. Furthermore, I
think that that's just a pile of shit. Do you believe it
yourself?

This brought a shocked silence. It should be noted
that I was not being profane purely for the sake of being

profane, I was doing this purposefully. If I had responded in a tactful way, saying, "Well, I don't quite understand what you mean, "we would have been off for a ride around the rhetorical ranch for the next thirty days. Here profanity became literally an up-against-the-wall bulldozer.

From there we went off to creative welfare. "Creative welfare" seemed to have to do with "since whites stole Indians' lands, all Indians' welfare payments are really installment payments due to them and it's not really welfare or charity." Well, that took us another five or ten minutes, and we kept breaking through one "creative" rationalization after another until finally we got down to the issue of organization.

An interesting aftermath is that some of this was filmed by the National Film Board of Canada, which was doing a series of documentaries on my work, and a film with part of this episode was shown at a meeting of Canadian development workers, with a number of these Indians present. The white Canadian community development workers kept looking at the floor, very embarrassed, during the unreeling of that scene, and giving sidelong looks at the Indians. After it was over one of the Indians stood up and said, "When Mr. Alinsky told us we were full of shit, that was the first time a white man has really talked to us as equals—you would never say that to us. You would always say 'Well, I can see your point of view but I'm a little confused,' and stuff like that. In other words you treat us as children."

Learn to search out the rationalizations, treat them as rationalizations, and break through. Do not make the mistake of locking yourself up in conflict with them as though they were the issues or problems with which you are trying to engage the local people.

THE PROCESS OF POWER

From the moment the organizer enters a community he
lives, dreams, eats, breathes, sleeps only one thing and
that is to build the mass power base of what he calls the
army. Until he has developed that mass power base, he
confronts no major issues. He has nothing with which to
confront anything. Until he has those means and power
instruments, his "tactics" are very different from power
tactics. Therefore, every move revolves around one central
point: how many recruits will this bring into the organization, whether by means of local organizations, churches,
service groups, labor unions, corner gangs, or as individuals. The only issue is, how will this increase the strength
of the organization. If by losing in a certain action he can
get more members than by winning, then victory lies in
losing and he will lose.

Change comes from power, and power comes from
organization. In order to act, people must get together.

Power is the reason for being of organizations. When
people agree on certain religious ideas and want the power
to propagate their faith, they organize and call it a church.
When people agree on certain political ideas and want
the power to put them into practice, they organize and
call it a political party. The same reason holds across the
board. Power and organization are one and the same.

The organizer knows, for example, that his biggest
job is to give the people the feeling that they can do something, that while they may accept the idea that organization means power, they have to experience this idea in

action. The organizer's job is to begin to build confidence and hope in the idea of organization and thus in the people themselves: to win limited victories, each of which will build confidence and the feeling that "if we can do so much with what we have now just think what we will be able to do when we get big and strong." It is almost like taking a prize-fighter up the road to the championship —you have to very carefully and selectively pick his opponents, knowing full well that certain defeats would be demoralizing and end his career. Sometimes the organizer may find such despair among the people that he has to put on a cinch fight.

An example occurred in the early days of Back of the Yards, the first community that I attempted to organize. This neighborhood was utterly demoralized. The people had no confidence in themselves or in their neighbors or in their cause. So we staged a cinch fight. One of the major problems in Back of the Yards in those days was an extraordinarily high rate of infant mortality. Some years earlier, the neighborhood had had the services of the Infant Welfare Society medical clinics. But about ten or fifteen years before I came to the neighborhood the Infant Welfare Society had been expelled because tales were spread that its personnel was disseminating birth-control information. The churches therefore drove out these "agents of sin." But soon the people were desperately in need of infant medical services. They had forgotten that they themselves had expelled the Infant Welfare Society from the Back of the Yards community.

After checking it out, I found out that all we had to do to get Infant Welfare Society medical services back into the neighborhood was ask for it. However, I kept this information to myself. We called an emergency meeting,

recommended we go in committee to the society's offices
and demand medical services. Our strategy was to prevent
the officials from saying anything; to start banging on
the desk and demanding that we get the services, *never*
permitting them to interrupt us or make any statement.
The only time we would let them talk was after we got
through. With this careful indoctrination we stormed into
the Infant Welfare Society downtown, identified ourselves,
and began a tirade consisting of militant demands, refus-
ing to permit them to say anything. All the time the poor
woman was desperately trying to say, "Why of course you
can have it. We'll start immediately." But she never had
a chance to say anything and finally we ended up in a
storm of "And we will not take 'No' for an answer!" At
which point she said, "Well, I've been trying to tell
you . . ." and I cut in, demanding, "Is it yes or is it no?"
She said, "Well of course it's yes." I said, "That's all we
wanted to know." And we stormed out of the place. All
the way back to Back of the Yards you could hear the
members of the committee saying, "Well, that's the way to
get things done: you just tell them off and don't give them
a chance to say anything. If we could get this with just
the few people that we have in the organization now, just
imagine what we can get when we have a big organization." (I suggest that before critics look upon this as "trick-
ery," they reflect on the discussion of means and ends.)

The organizer simultaneously carries on many functions as he analyzes, attacks, and disrupts the prevailing
power pattern. The ghetto or slum in which he is organizing is *not* a disorganized community. There is no such
animal as a disorganized community. It is a contradiction
in terms to use the two words "disorganization" and "community" together: the word community itself means an

organized, communal life; people living in an organized fashion. The people in the community may have experienced successive frustrations to the point that their will to participate has seemed to atrophy. They may be living in anonymity and may be starved for personal recognition. They may be suffering from various forms of deprivation and discrimination. They may have accepted anonymity and resigned in apathy. They may despair that their children will inherit a somewhat better world. From your point of view they may have a very negative form of existence, but the fact is that they are organized in that way of life. Call it organized apathy or organized nonparticipation, but that is their community pattern. They are living under a certain set of arrangements, standards, way of life. They may in short have surrendered—but life goes on in an organized form, with a definite power structure; even if it is, as Thoreau called most lives, "quiet desperation."

Therefore, if your function is to attack apathy and get people to participate it is necessary to attack the prevailing patterns of organized living in the community. *The first step in community organization is community disorganization.* The disruption of the present organization is the first step toward community organization. Present arrangements must be disorganized if they are to be displaced by new patterns that provide the opportunities and means for citizen participation. *All change means disorganization of the old and organization of the new.*

This is why the organizer is immediately confronted with conflict. The organizer dedicated to changing the life of a particular community must first rub raw the resentments of the people of the community; fan the latent hostilities of many of the people to the point of overt expression. He must search out controversy and issues, rather

than avoid them, for unless there is controversy people
are not concerned enough to act. The use of the adjective
"controversial" to qualify the word "issue" is a meaningless
redundancy. There can be no such thing as a "non-con-
troversial" issue. When there is agreement there is no
issue; issues only arise when there is disagreement or
controversy. An organizer must stir up dissatisfaction and
discontent; provide a channel into which the people can
angrily pour their frustrations. He must create a mechanism that can drain off the underlying guilt for having
accepted the previous situation for so long a time. Out of
this mechanism, a new community organization arises.
But more on this point later.

The job then is getting the people to move, to act, to
participate; in short, to develop and harness the necessary
power to effectively conflict with the prevailing patterns
and change them. When those prominent in the status
quo turn and label you an "agitator" they are completely
correct, for that is, in one word, your function—to agitate
to the point of conflict.

A sound analogy is to be found in the organization of
trade unions. A competent union organizer approaches his
objective, let's say the organization of a particular industrial plant where the workers are underpaid, suffering
from discriminatory practices, and without job security.
The workers accept these conditions as inevitable, and
they express their demoralization by saying, "what's the
use." In private they resent these circumstances, complain,
talk about the futility of "bucking the big shots" and generally succumb to frustration—*all because of the lack of
opportunity for effective action.*

Enter the labor organizer or the agitator. He begins
his "trouble making" by stirring up these angers, frustra-

tions, and resentments, and highlighting specific issues or grievances that heighten controversy. He dramatizes the injustices by describing conditions at other industrial plants engaged in the same kind of work where the workers are far better off economically and have better working conditions, job security, health benefits, and pensions as well as other advantages that had not even been thought of by the workers he is trying to organize. Just as important, he points out that the workers in the other places had also been exploited in the past and had existed under similar circumstances until they used their intelligence and energies to organize into a power instrument known as a trade union, with the result that they achieved all of these other benefits. Generally this approach results in the formation of a new trade union.

Let us examine what this labor organizer has done. He has taken a group of apathetic workers; he has fanned their resentments and hostilities by a number of means, including challenging contrasts of better conditions of other workers in similar industries. Most important, he has demonstrated that something can be done, and that there is a concrete way of doing it that has already proven its effectiveness and success: that by organizing together as a trade union they will have the power and the instrument with which to make these changes. He now has the workers participating in a trade union and supporting its program. We must never forget that so long as there is no opportunity or method to make changes, it is senseless to get people agitated or angry, leaving them no course of action except to blow their tops.

And so the labor organizer simultaneously breeds conflict and builds a power structure. The war between the trade union and management is resolved either through a strike or a negotiation. Either method involves the use of power; the economic power of the strike or the threat of it, which results in successful negotiations. *No one can negotiate without the power to compel negotiation.*

This is the function of a community organizer. Anything otherwise is wishful non-thinking. To attempt to operate on a good-will rather than on a power basis would be to attempt something that the world has not yet experienced.

In the beginning the organizer's first job is to create the issues or problems. It sounds mad to say that a community such as a low-income ghetto or even a middle-class community has no issues per se. The reader may feel that this statement borders on lunacy, particularly with reference to low-income communities. The simple fact is that in any community, regardless of how poor, people may have serious problems—but they do not have issues, they have a bad scene. An issue is something you can do something about, but as long as you feel powerless and unable to do anything about it, all you have is a bad scene. The people resign themselves to a rationalization: it's that kind of world, it's a crumby world, we didn't ask to come into it but we are stuck with it and all we can do is hope that something happens somewhere, somehow, sometime. This is what is usually taken as apathy, what we discussed earlier—that policy follows power. Through action, persuasion, and communication the organizer makes it clear that organization will give them the power, the ability, the strength, the force to be able to do something about these particular problems. It is then that a bad scene begins to break up into specific issues, because now the people can do something about it. What the organizer does is convert the plight into a problem. The question is whether they do it this way or that way or whether they do all of it or part of it. But now you have issues.

The organization is born out of the issues and the issues are born out of the organization. They go together, they are concomitants essential to each other. Organizations are built on issues that are specific, immediate, and realizable.

Organizations must be based on many issues. Organizations need action as an individual needs oxygen. The cessation of action brings death to the organization through factionalism and inaction, through dialogues and conferences that are actually a form of rigor mortis rather than life. It is impossible to maintain constant action on a single issue. A single issue is a fatal strait jacket that will stifle the life of an organization. Furthermore, a single issue drastically limits your appeal, where multiple issues would draw in the many potential members essential to the building of a broad, mass-based organization. Each person has a hierarchy of desires or values; he may be sympathetic to your single issue but not concerned enough about that particular one to work and fight for it. Many issues mean many members. Communities are not economic organizations like labor unions, with specific economic issues; they are as complex as life itself.

To organize a community you must understand that in a highly mobile, urbanized society the word "community" means community of interests, *not* physical community. The exceptions are ethnic ghettos where segregation has resulted in physical communities that coincide with their community of interests, or, during political campaigns, political districts that are based on geographical demarcations.

People hunger for drama and adventure, for a breath

of life in a dreary, drab existence. One of a number of cartoons in my office shows two gum-chewing stenographers who have just left the movies. One is talking to the other, and says, "You know, Sadie. You know what the trouble with life is? There just ain't any background music."

But it's more than that. It is a desperate search for personal identity—to let other people know that at least you are alive. Let's take a common case in the ghetto. A man is living in a slum tenement. He doesn't know anybody and nobody knows him. He doesn't care for anyone because no one cares for him. On the corner newsstand are newspapers with pictures of people like Mayor Daley and other people from a different world—a world that he doesn't know, a world that doesn't know that he is even alive.

When the organizer approaches him part of what begins to be communicated is that through the organization and its power he will get his birth certificate for life, that he will become known, that things will change from the drabness of a life where all that changes is the calendar. This same man, in a demonstration at City Hall, might find himself confronting the mayor and saying, "Mr. Mayor, we have had it up to here and we are not going to take it any more." Television cameramen put their microphones in front of him and ask, "What is your name, sir?" "John Smith." Nobody ever asked him what his name was before. And then, "What do you think about this, Mr. Smith?" Nobody ever asked him what he thought about anything before. Suddenly he's alive! This is part of the adventure, part of what is so important to people in getting involved in organizational activities and what the organizer has to communicate to him. Not that every member will be giving his name on television—that's a bonus— but for once, because he is working together with a group, what he works for will mean something.

Let us look at what is called *process*. *Process* tells us *how*. *Purpose* tells us *why*. But in reality, it is academic to draw a line between them, they are part of a continuum. Process and purpose are so welded to each other that it is impossible to mark where one leaves off and the other begins, or which is which. The very process of democratic participation is for the purpose of organization rather than to rid the alleys of dirt. Process is really purpose.

Through all this the constant guiding star of the organizer is in those words, "The dignity of the individual." Working with this compass, he soon discovers many axioms of effective organization.

If you respect the dignity of the individual you are working with, then his desires, not yours; his values, not yours; his ways of working and fighting, not yours; his choice of leadership, not yours; his programs, not yours, are important and must be followed; except if his programs violate the high values of a free and open society. For example, take the question, "What if the program of the local people offends the rights of other groups, for reasons of color, religion, economic status, or politics? Should this program be accepted just because it is their program?" The answer is categorically no. Always remember that "the guiding star is 'the dignity of the individual.'" This is the purpose of the program. Obviously any program that opposes people because of race, religion, creed, or economic status, is the antithesis of the fundamental dignity of the individual.

It is difficult for people to believe that you really respect their dignity. After all, they know very few people, including their own neighbors, who do. But it is equally difficult for you to surrender that little image of God created in our own likeness, which lurks in all of us and tells us that we secretly believe that we know what's best for the people. A successful organizer has learned emotionally as well as intellectually to respect the dignity of the people with whom he is working. Thus an effective organizational experience is as much an educational process for the organizer as it is for the people with whom he is working. They both must learn to respect the dignity of the individual, and they both must learn that in the last analysis this is the basic purpose of organization, for participation is the heartbeat of the democratic way of life.

We learn, when we respect the dignity of the people, that they cannot be denied the elementary right to participate fully in the solutions to their own problems. Self-respect arises only out of people who play an active role in solving their own crises and who are not helpless, passive, puppet-like recipients of private or public services. To give people help, while denying them a significant part in the action, contributes nothing to the development of the individual. In the deepest sense it is not giving but taking—taking their dignity. Denial of the opportunity for participation is the denial of human dignity and democracy. It will not work.

In *Reveille for Radicals* I described an incident in which the government of Mexico once decided to pay tribute to Mexican mothers. A proclamation was issued that every mother whose sewing machine was being held by the Monte de Piedad (the national pawn shop of Mexico) should have her machine returned as a gift on Mother's Day. There was tremendous joy over the occasion. Here was a gift being made outright, without any participation on the part of the recipients. *Inside of three weeks the exact same number of sewing machines was back in the pawn shop.*

Another example occurred in a statement made by the United Nations delegate from Liberia. Analyzing problems of Liberia, he noted that his nation had been deprived of "the benefits of a previous history of colonialism." Press reaction was astonishment and ridicule, but the statement showed insight and wisdom. The people of Liberia had never been exploited by a colonial power, never been forced to band together at the risk of great personal sacrifice to revolt for freedom. They had been given "freedom" upon the establishment of their nation. Even freedom, as a gift, is deficient in dignity; hence the political sterility of Liberia.

As Finley Peter Dunne's Mr. Dooley put it,

> Don't ask f'r rights. Take thim. An' don't let anny wan give thim to ye. A right that is handed to ye fer nawthin has somethin the mather with it. It's more thin likely it's only a wrrong turned inside out.

The organization has to be used in every possible sense as an educational mechanism, but education is not propaganda. Real education is the means by which the membership will begin to make sense out of their relationship as individuals to the organization and to the world they live in, so that they can make informed and intelligent judgments. The stream of activities and programs of the organization provides a never-ending series of *specific* issues and situations that create a rich field for the learning process.

The concern and conflict about each specific issue

leads to a speedily enlarging area of interest. Competent organizers should be sensitive to these opportunities. Without the learning process, the building of an organization becomes simply the substitution of one power group for another.

Tactics

We will either find a way or make one.

— **HANNIBAL**

TACTICS MEANS doing what you can with what you have. Tactics are those consciously deliberate acts by which human beings live with each other and deal with the world around them. In the world of give and take, tactics is the art of how to take and how to give. Here our concern is with the tactic of taking; how the Have-Nots can take power away from the Haves.

For an elementary illustration of tactics, take parts of your face as the point of reference; your eyes, your ears, and your nose. First the eyes; if you have organized a vast, mass-based people's organization, you can parade it visibly before the enemy and openly show your power. Second the ears; if your organization is small in numbers, then do what Gideon did: conceal the members in the dark but raise a din and clamor that will make the listener believe that your organization numbers many more than it does. Third, the nose; if your organization is too tiny even for noise, stink up the place.

Always remember the first rule of power tactics:

*Power is not only what you have but what the enemy
thinks you have.*°

The second rule is: *Never go outside the experience
of your people.* When an action or tactic is outside the
experience of the people, the result is confusion, fear, and
retreat. It also means a collapse of communication, as we
have noted.

The third rule is: *Wherever possible go outside of
the experience of the enemy.* Here you want to cause
confusion, fear, and retreat.

General William T. Sherman, whose name still causes
a frenzied reaction throughout the South, provided a
classic example of going outside the enemy's experience.
Until Sherman, military tactics and strategies were based
on standard patterns. All armies had fronts, rears, flanks,
lines of communication, and lines of supply. Military campaigns were aimed at such standard objectives as rolling
up the flanks of the enemy army or cutting the lines of
supply or lines of communication, or moving around to
attack from the rear. When Sherman cut loose on his
famous March to the Sea, he had no front or rear lines of
supplies or any other lines. He was on the loose and
living on the land. The South, confronted with this new
form of military invasion, reacted with confusion, panic,
terror, and collapse. Sherman swept on to inevitable vic-

° Power has always derived from two main sources, money and people.
Lacking money, the Have-Nots must build power from their own flesh
and blood. A mass movement expresses itself with mass tactics. Against
the finesse and sophistication of the status quo, the Have-Nots have
always had to club their way. In early Renaissance Italy the playing
cards showed swords for the nobility (the word *spade* is a corruption
of the Italian word for sword), chalices (which became hearts) for the
clergy, diamonds for the merchants, and clubs as the symbol of the
peasants.

tory. It was the same tactic that, years later in the early days of World War II, the Nazi Panzer tank divisions emulated in their far-flung sweeps into enemy territory, as did our own General Patton with the American Third Armored Division.

The fourth rule is: *Make the enemy live up to their own book of rules.* You can kill them with this, for they can no more obey their own rules than the Christian church can live up to Christianity.

The fourth rule carries within it the fifth rule: *Ridicule is man's most potent weapon.* It is almost impossible to counterattack ridicule. Also it infuriates the opposition, who then react to your advantage.

The sixth rule is: *A good tactic is one that your people enjoy.*° If your people are not having a ball doing it, there is something very wrong with the tactic.

The seventh rule: *A tactic that drags on too long becomes a drag.* Man can sustain militant interest in any issue for only a limited time, after which it becomes a ritualistic commitment, like going to church on Sunday mornings. New issues and crises are always developing, and one's reaction becomes, "Well, my heart bleeds for those people and I'm all for the boycott, but after all there are other important things in life"—and there it goes.

The eighth rule: *Keep the pressure on,* with different tactics and actions, and utilize all events of the period for your purpose.

° Alinsky takes the iconoclast's pleasure in kicking the biggest behinds in town and the sport is not untempting . . ." —William F. Buckley, Jr., *Chicago Daily News,* October 19, 1966.

The ninth rule: *The threat is usually more terrifying than the thing itself.*

The tenth rule: *The major premise for tactics is the development of operations that will maintain a constant pressure upon the opposition.* It is this unceasing pressure that results in the reactions from the opposition that are essential for the success of the campaign. It should be remembered not only that the action is in the reaction but that action is itself the consequence of reaction and of reaction to the reaction, ad infinitum. The pressure produces the reaction, and constant pressure sustains action.

The eleventh rule is: *If you push a negative hard and deep enough it will break through into its counterside;* this is based on the principle that every positive has its negative. We have already seen the conversion of the negative into the positive, in Mahatma Gandhi's development of the tactic of passive resistance.

One corporation we organized against responded to the continuous application of pressure by burglarizing my home, and then using the keys taken in the burglary to burglarize the offices of the Industrial Areas Foundation where I work. The panic in this corporation was clear from the nature of the burglaries, for nothing was taken in either burglary to make it seem that the thieves were interested in ordinary loot—they took only the records that applied to the corporation. Even the most amateurish burglar would have had more sense than to do what the private detective agency hired by that corporation did. The police departments in California and Chicago agreed that "the corporation might just as well have left its fingerprints all over the place."

In a fight almost anything goes. It almost reaches the

point where you stop to apologize if a chance blow lands *above* the belt. When a corporation bungles like the one that burglarized my home and office, my visible public reaction is shock, horror, and moral outrage. In this case, we let it be known that sooner or later it would be confronted with this crime as well as with a whole series of other derelictions, before a United States Senate Subcommittee Investigation. Once sworn in, with congressional immunity, we would make these actions public. This threat, plus the fact that an attempt on my life had been made in Southern California, had the corporation on a spot where it would be publicly suspect in the event of assassination. At one point I found myself in a thirty-room motel in which every other room was occupied by their security men. This became another devil in the closet to haunt this corporation and to keep the pressure on.

The twelfth rule: *The price of a successful attack is a constructive alternative.* You cannot risk being trapped by the enemy in his sudden agreement with your demand and saying "You're right—we don't know what to do about this issue. Now you tell us."

The thirteenth rule: *Pick the target, freeze it, personalize it, and polarize it.*

In conflict tactics there are certain rules that the organizer should always regard as universalities. One is that the opposition must be singled out as the target and "frozen." By this I mean that in a complex, interrelated, urban society, it becomes increasingly difficult to single out who is to blame for any particular evil. There is a constant, and somewhat legitimate, passing of the buck. In these times of urbanization, complex metropolitan governments, the complexities of major interlocked corporations, and the interlocking of political life between cities and counties and metropolitan authorities, the problem that threatens to loom more and more is that of identifying the enemy. Obviously there is no point to tactics unless one has a target upon which to center the attacks. One big problem is a constant shifting of responsibility from one jurisdiction to another—individuals and bureaus one after another disclaim responsibility for particular conditions, attributing the authority for any change to some other force. In a corporation one gets the situation where the president of the corporation says that he does not have the responsibility, it is up to the board of trustees or the board of directors, the board of directors can shift it over to the stockholders, etc., etc. And the same thing goes, for example, on the Board of Education appointments in the city of Chicago, where an extra-legal committee is empowered to make selections of nominees for the board and the mayor then uses his legal powers to select names from that list. When the mayor is attacked for not having any blacks on the list, he shifts the responsibility over to the committee, pointing out that he has to select those names from a list submitted by the committee, and if the list is all white, then he has no responsibility. The committee can shift the responsibility back by pointing out that it is the mayor who has the authority to select the names, and so it goes in a comic (if it were not so tragic) routine of "who's on first" or "under which shell is the pea hidden?"

The same evasion of responsibility is to be found in all areas of life and other areas of City Hall Urban Renewal departments, who say the responsibility is over here, and somebody else says the responsibility is over there, the city says it is a state responsibility, and the state says it is a federal responsibility and the federal government passes it back to the local community, and on ad infinitum.

It should be borne in mind that the target is always trying to shift responsibility to get out of being the target. There is a constant squirming and moving and strategy—purposeful, and malicious at times, other times just for straight self-survival—on the part of the designated target. The forces for change must keep this in mind and pin that target down securely. If an organization permits responsibility to be diffused and distributed in a number of areas, attack becomes impossible.

I remember specifically that when the Woodlawn Organization started the campaign against public school segregation, both the superintendent of schools and the chairman of the Board of Education vehemently denied any racist segregationist practices in the Chicago Public School System. They took the position that they did not even have any racial-identification data in their files, so they did not know which of their students were black and which were white. As for the fact that we had all-white schools and all-black schools, well, that's just the way it was.

If we had been confronted with a politically sophisticated school superintendent he could have very well replied, "Look, when I came to Chicago the city school system was following, as it is now, a neighborhood school policy. Chicago's neighborhoods are segregated. There are white neighborhoods and black neighborhoods and therefore you have white schools and black schools. Why attack me? Why not attack the segregated neighborhoods and change them?" He would have had a valid point, of sorts; I still shiver when I think of this possibility; but the segregated neighborhoods would have passed the buck to someone else and so it would have gone into a dog-chasing-his-tail pattern—and it would have been a fifteen-year job to try to break down the segregated residential pattern of Chicago. We did not have the power to start that kind of a conflict. One of the criteria in picking your target is the target's vulnerability—where do you have the power to start? Furthermore, any target can always say, "Why do you center on me when there are others to blame as well?" When you "freeze the target," you disregard these arguments and, for the moment, all the others to blame.

Then, as you zero in and freeze your target and carry out your attack, all of the "others" come out of the woodwork very soon. They become visible by their support of the target.

The other important point in the choosing of a target is that it must be a personification, not something general and abstract such as a community's segregated practices or a major corporation or City Hall. It is not possible to develop the necessary hostility against, say, City Hall, which after all is a concrete, physical, inanimate structure, or against a corporation, which has no soul or identity, or a public school administration, which again is an inanimate system.

John L. Lewis, the leader of the radical C.I.O. labor organization in the 1930s, was fully aware of this, and as a consequence the C.I.O. never attacked General Motors, they always attacked its president, Alfred "Icewater-In-His-Veins" Sloan; they never attacked the Republic Steel Corporation but always its president, "Bloodied Hands" Tom Girdler, and so with us when we attacked the then-superintendent of the Chicago public school system, Benjamin Willis. Let nothing get you off your target.

With this focus comes a polarization. As we have indicated before, all issues must be polarized if action is to follow. The classic statement on polarization comes from

Christ: "He that is not with me is against me" (Luke 11:23). He allowed no middle ground to the money-changers in the Temple. One acts decisively only in the conviction that all the angels are on one side and all the devils on the other. A leader may struggle toward a decision and weigh the merits and demerits of a situation which is 52 per cent positive and 48 per cent negative, but once the decision is reached he must assume that his cause is 100 per cent positive and the opposition 100 per cent negative. He can't toss forever in limbo, and avoid decision. He can't weigh arguments or reflect endlessly—he must decide and act. Otherwise there are Hamlet's words:

> And thus the native hue of resolution
> Is sicklied o'er with the pale cast of thought,
> And enterprises of great pith and moment
> With this regard their currents turn awry,
> And lose the name of action.

Many liberals, during our attack on the then-school superintendent, were pointing out that after all he wasn't a 100 per cent devil, he was a regular churchgoer, he was a good family man, and he was generous in his contributions to charity. Can you imagine in the arena of conflict charging that so-and-so is a racist bastard and then diluting the impact of the attack with qualifying remarks such as "He is a good churchgoing man, generous to charity, and a good husband"? This becomes political idiocy.

An excellent illustration of the importance of polarization here was cited by Ruth McKenney in *Industrial Valley,* her classical study of the beginning of organization of the rubber workers in Akron, Ohio:

> [John L.] Lewis faced the mountaineer workers
> of Akron calmly. He had taken the trouble to pre-

pare himself with exact information about the rubber industry and The Goodyear Tire and Rubber Company. He made no vague, general speech, the kind the rubberworkers were used to hearing from Green [then president of the A.F. of L.]. Lewis named names and quoted figures. His audience was startled and pleased when he called Cliff Slusser by name, described him, and finally denounced him. The A.F. of L. leaders who used to come into Akron in the old days were generally doing well if they remembered who Paul Litchfield was.

The Lewis speech was a battle cry, a challenge. He started off by recalling the vast profits the rubber companies had always made, even during the deepest days of the Depression. He mentioned the Goodyear labor policy, and quoted Mr. Litchfield's pious opinions about the partnership of labor and capital.

"What," he said in his deep, passionate voice, "have Goodyear workers gotten out of the growth of the company?" His audience squirmed in its seats, listening with almost painful fervor.

"Partnership!" he sneered. "Well, labor and capital may be partners in theory, *but they are enemies in fact.*"

. . . The rubberworkers listened to this with surprise and great excitement. William Green used to tell them about the partnership of labor and capital nearly as eloquently as Paul Litchfield. Here was a man who put into words—what eloquent and educated and even elegant words— facts they knew to be true from their own experience. Here was a man who said things that made real sense to a guy who worked on a tire machine at Goodyear.

"Organize!" Lewis shouted, and his voice echoed from the beams of the armory. "Organize!" he said, pounding the speaking pulpit until it jumped. "Organize! Go to Goodyear and tell them you want some of those stock dividends. Say, So we're supposed to be partners, are we? Well, we're not. *We're enemies.*"

- *The real action is in the enemy's reaction.*
- *The enemy properly goaded and guided in his reaction will be your major strength.*
- *Tactics, like organization, like life, require that you move with the action.*

The scene is Rochester, New York, the home of Eastman Kodak—or rather Eastman Kodak, the home of Rochester, New York. Rochester is literally dominated by this industrial giant. For anyone to fight or publicly challenge Kodak is in itself completely outside of Rochester's experience. Even to this day this company does not have a labor union. Its attitudes toward the general public make paternalistic feudalism look like participatory democracy.

Rochester prides itself on being one of America's cultural crown jewels; it has its libraries, school system, university, museums, and its well-known symphony. As previously mentioned we were coming in on the invitation of the black ghetto to organize them (they literally organized to invite us in). The city was in a state of hysteria and fear at the very mention of my name. Whatever I did was news. Even my old friend and tutor, John L. Lewis, called me and affectionately growled, "I resent the fact that you are more hated in Rochester than I was." This was the setting.

One of the first times I arrived at the airport I was surrounded by reporters from the media. The first question was what I thought about Rochester as a city and I replied,

"It is a huge southern plantation transplanted north." To the question why was I "meddling" in the black ghetto after "everything" that Eastman Kodak had done for the blacks (there had been a bloody riot, National Guard, etc., the previous summer), I looked blank and replied, "Maybe I am innocent and uninformed of what has been happening here, but as far as I know the only thing Eastman Kodak has done on the race issue in America has been to introduce color film." The reaction was shock, anger, and resentment from Kodak. They were not being attacked or insulted—they were being laughed at, and this was insufferable. It was the first dart tossed at the big bull. Soon Eastman would become so angry that it would make the kind of charges that finally led to its own downfall.

The next question was about my response to a bitter personal denunciation of me from W. Allen Wallis, the president of the University of Rochester and a present director of Eastman Kodak. He had been the head of the Department of Business Administration, formerly, at the University of Chicago. He was at the university when it was locked in bitter warfare with the black organization in Woodlawn. "Wallis?" I replied. "Which one are you talking about—Wallace of Alabama, or Wallis of Rochester—but I guess there isn't any difference, so what was your question?" This reply (1) introduced an element of ridicule and (2) it ended any further attacks from the president of the University of Rochester, who began to suspect that he was going to be shafted with razors, and that an encounter with me or with my associates was not going to be an academic dialogue.

It should be remembered that you can threaten the enemy and get away with it. You can insult and annoy

him, but the one thing that is unforgivable and that is
certain to get him to react is to laugh at him. This causes
an irrational anger.

I hesitate to spell out specific applications of these
tactics. I remember an unfortunate experience with my
Reveille for Radicals, in which I collected accounts of
particular actions and tactics employed in organizing a
number of communities. For some time after the book was
published I got reports that would-be organizers were
using this book as a manual, and whenever they were confronted with a puzzling situation they would retreat into
some vestibule or alley and thumb through to find the
answer! There can be no prescriptions for particular
situations because the same situation rarely recurs, any
more than history repeats itself. People, pressures, and
patterns of power are variables, and a particular combination exists only in a particular time—even then the variables are constantly in a state of flux. Tactics must be
understood as specific applications of the rules and principles that I have listed above. It is the *principles* that the
organizer must carry with him in battle. To these he
applies his imagination, and he relates them tactically to
specific situations.

For example, I have emphasized and re-emphasized
that tactics means you do what you can with what you've
got, and that power in the main has always gravitated
towards those who have money and those whom people
follow. The resources of the Have-Nots are (1) no money
and (2) lots of people. All right, let's start from there.
People can show their power by voting. What else? Well,
they have physical bodies. How can they use them? Now
a melange of ideas begins to appear. Use the power of the
law by making the establishment obey its own rules. Go

outside the experience of the enemy, stay inside the experience of your people. Emphasize tactics that your people will enjoy. The threat is usually more terrifying than the tactic itself. Once all these rules and principles are festering in your imagination they grow into a synthesis.

I suggested that we might buy one hundred seats for one of Rochester's symphony concerts. We would select a concert in which the music was relatively quiet. The hundred blacks who would be given the tickets would first be treated to a three-hour pre-concert dinner in the community, in which they would be fed nothing but baked beans, and lots of them; then the people would go to the symphony hall—with obvious consequences. Imagine the scene when the action began! The concert would be over before the first movement! (If this be a Freudian slip—so be it!)

Let's examine this tactic in terms of the concepts mentioned above.

First, the disturbance would be utterly outside the experience of the establishment, which was expecting the usual stuff of mass meetings, street demonstrations, confrontations and parades. Not in their wildest fears would they expect an attack on their prize cultural jewel, their famed symphony orchestra. Second, all of the action would ridicule and make a farce of the law for there is no law, and there probably never will be, banning natural physical functions. Here you would have a combination not only of noise but also of odor, what you might call natural stink bombs. Regular stink bombs are illegal and cause for immediate arrest, but there would be absolutely nothing here that the Police Department or the ushers or any other servants of the establishment could do about it. The law would be completely paralyzed.

People would recount what had happened in the symphony hall and the reaction of the listener would be to crack up in laughter. It would make the Rochester Symphony and the establishment look utterly ridiculous. There would be no way for the authorities to cope with any future attacks of a similar character. What could they do? Demand that people not eat baked beans before coming to a concert? Ban anyone from succumbing to natural urges during the concert? Announce to the world that concerts must not be interrupted by farting? Such talk would destroy the future of the symphony season. Imagine the tension at the opening of any concert! Imagine the feeling of the conductor as he raised his baton!

With this would come certain fall-outs. On the following morning, the matrons, to whom the symphony season is one of the major social functions, would confront their husbands (both executives and junior executives) at the breakfast table and say, "John, we are not going to have our symphony season ruined by *those people!* I don't know what they want but whatever it is, something has got to be done and this kind of thing has to be stopped!"

Lastly, we have the universal rule that while one goes outside the experience of the enemy in order to induce confusion and fear, one must not do the same with one's own people, because you do not want them to be confused and fearful. Now, let us examine this rule with reference to the symphony tactic. To start with, the tactic is within the experience of the local people; it also satisfies another rule—that the people must enjoy the tactic. Here we have an ambivalent situation. The reaction of the blacks in the ghetto—their laughter when the tactic was proposed—made it clear that the tactic, at least in fantasy, was within their experience. It connected with their hatred of Whitey. The one thing that all oppressed people want to do to their oppressors is shit on them. Here was an approximate way to do this. However, we were also aware that when they found themselves actually in the symphony hall, probably for the first time in their lives, they would find themselves seated amid a mass of whites, many of them in formal dress. The situation would be so much *out of their experience* that they might congeal and revert back to their previous role. The very idea of doing what they had come to do would be so embarrassing, so mortifying, that they would do almost anything to avoid carrying through the plan. But we also knew that the baked beans would compel them physically to go through with the tactic regardless of how they felt.

I must emphasize that tactics like this are not just cute; any organizer knows, as a particular tactic grows out of the rules and principles of revolution, that he must always analyze the merit of the tactic and determine its strengths and weaknesses in terms of these same rules.

Imagine the scene in the U.S. Courtroom in Chicago's recent conspiracy trial of the seven if the defendants and counsel had anally trumpeted their contempt for Judge Hoffman and the system. What could Judge Hoffman, the bailiffs, or anyone else, do? Would the judge have found them in contempt for farting? Here was a tactic for which there was no legal precedent. The press reaction would have stunk up the judge for the rest of time.

Another tactic involving the bodily functions developed in Chicago during the days of the Johnson-Goldwater campaign. Commitments that were made by the authorities to the Woodlawn ghetto organization were not being met by the city. The political threat that had originally

compelled these commitments was no longer operative.
The community organization had no alternative but to
support Johnson and therefore the Democratic administration felt the political threat had evaporated. It must be
remembered here that not only is pressure essential to
compel the establishment to make its initial concession,
but the pressure must be maintained to make the establishment deliver. The second factor seemed to be lost to the
Woodlawn Organization.

Since the organization was blocked in the political
arena, new tactics and a new arena had to be devised.

O'Hare Airport became the target. To begin with,
O'Hare is the world's busiest airport. Think for a moment
of the common experience of jet travelers. Your stewardess
brings you your lunch or dinner. After eating, most people
want to go to the lavatory. However, this is often inconvenient because your tray and those of your seat partners are loaded down with dishes. So you wait until the
stewardess has removed the trays. By that time those who
are seated closest to the lavatory have got up and the
"occupied" sign is on. So you wait. And in these days of
jet travel the seat belt sign is soon flashed, as the airplane
starts its landing approach. You decide to wait until after
landing and use the facilities in the terminal. This is
obvious to anyone who watches the unloading of passengers at various gates in any airport—many of the passengers are making a beeline for the men's or the ladies' room.

With this in mind, the tactic becomes obvious—we
tie up the lavoratories. In the restrooms you drop a dime,
enter, push the lock on the door—and you can stay there
all day. Therefore the occupation of the sit-down toilets
presents no problem. It would take just a relatively few
people to walk into these cubicles, armed with books and

newspapers, lock the doors, and tie up all the facilities. What are the police going to do? Break in and demand evidence of legitimate occupancy? Therefore, the ladies' restrooms could be occupied completely; the only problem in the men's lavatories would be the stand-up urinals. This, too, could be taken care of, by having groups busy themselves around the airport and then move in on the stand-up urinals to line up four or five deep whenever a flight arrived. An intelligence study was launched to learn how many sit-down toilets for both men and women, as well as stand-up urinals, there were in the entire O'Hare Airport complex and how many men and women would be necessary for the nation's first "shit-in."

The consequences of this kind of action would be catastrophic in many ways. People would be desperate for a place to relieve themselves. One can see children yelling at their parents, "Mommy, I've got to go," and desperate mothers surrendering, "All right—well, do it. Do it right here." O'Hare would soon become a shambles. The whole scene would become unbelievable and the laughter and ridicule would be nationwide. It would probably get a front page story in the London *Times*. It would be a source of great mortification and embarrassment to the city administration. It might even create the kind of emergency in which planes would have to be held up while passengers got back aboard to use the plane's toilet facilities.

The threat of this tactic was leaked (again there may be a Freudian slip here, and again, so what?) back to the administration, and within forty-eight hours the Wood-lawn Organization found itself in conference with the authorities who said that they were certainly going to live up to their commitments and they could never understand where anyone got the idea that a promise made by Chicago's City Hall would not be observed. At no point, then or since, has there ever been any open mention of the threat of the O'Hare tactic. Very few of the members of the Woodlawn Organization knew how close they were to writing history.

With the universal principle that the right things are always done for the wrong reasons and the tactical rule that negatives become positives, we can understand the following examples.

In its early history the organized black ghetto in the Woodlawn neighborhood in Chicago engaged in conflict with the slum landlords. It never picketed the local slum tenements or the landlord's office. It selected its blackest blacks and bused them out to the lily-white suburb of the slum landlord's residence. Their picket signs, which said, "Did you know that Jones, your neighbor, is a slum landlord?" were completely irrelevant; the point was that the pickets knew Jones would be inundated with phone calls from his neighbors.

JONES: Before you say a word let me tell you that those signs are a bunch of lies!
NEIGHBOR: Look, Jones, I don't give a damn what you do for a living. All we know is that you get those goddam niggers out of here or you get out!

Jones came out and signed.

The pressure that gave us our positive power was the negative of racism in a white society. We exploited it for our own purposes.

Let us take one of the negative stereotypes that so many whites have of blacks: that blacks like to sit around eating watermelon. Suppose that 3,000 blacks suddenly descended into the downtown sections of any city, each armed with and munching a huge piece of watermelon. This spectacle would be so far outside the experience of the whites that they would be unnerved and disorganized. In alarm over what the blacks were up to, the establishment would probably react to the advantage of the blacks. Furthermore, the whites would recognize at last the absurdity of their stereotype of black habits. Whites would squirm in embarrassment, knowing that they were being ridiculed. That would be the end of the black watermelon stereotype. I think that this tactic would bring the administration to contact black leadership and ask what their demands were even if no demands had been made. Here again is a case of doing what you can with what you've got.

Another example of doing what you can with what you've got is the following:

> I was lecturing at a college run by a very conservative, almost fundamentalist Protestant denomination. Afterward some of the students came to my motel to talk to me. Their problem was that they couldn't have any fun on campus. They weren't permitted to dance or smoke or have a can of beer. I had been talking about the strategy of effecting change in a society and they wanted to know what tactics they could use to change their situation. I reminded them that a tactic is doing what you can with what you've got. "Now, what have you got?" I asked. "What do they permit you to do?" "Practically nothing," they said, "except—you know—we can chew gum." I said, "Fine. Gum becomes the weapon. You get two or three hundred students to get two packs of gum each, which is quite a wad. Then you have them drop it on the campus walks. This will cause absolute chaos. Why, with five hundred wads of

gum I could paralyze Chicago, stop all the traffic in the Loop." They looked at me as though I was some kind of a nut. But about two weeks later I got an ecstatic letter saying, "It worked! It worked! Now we can do just about anything so long as we don't chew gum."

—quoted in Marion K. Sanders' *The Professional Radical—Conversations with Saul Alinsky.*

As with the slum landlords, one of the major department stores in the nation was brought to heel by the following threatened tactic. Remember the rule—the threat is often more effective than the tactic itself, but *only* if you are so organized that the establishment knows not only that you have the power to execute the tactic but that you definitely will. You can't do much bluffing in this game; if you're ever caught bluffing, forget about ever using threats in the future. On that point you're dead.

There is a particular department store that happens to cater to the carriage trade. It attracts many customers on the basis of its labels as well as the quality of its merchandise. Because of this, economic boycotts had failed to deter even the black middle class from shopping there. At the time its employment policies were more restrictive than those of the other stores. Blacks were hired for only the most menial jobs.

We made up a tactic. A busy Saturday shopping date was selected. Approximately 3,000 blacks all dressed up in their good churchgoing suits or dresses would be bused downtown. When you put 3,000 blacks on the main floor of a store, even one that covers a square block, suddenly the entire color of the store changes. Any white coming through the revolving doors would take one pop-eyed look and assume that somehow he had stepped into Africa. He would keep right on going out of the store. This would end the white trade for the day.

For a low-income group, shopping is a time-consuming experience, for economy means everything. This would mean that every counter would be occupied by potential customers, carefully examining the quality of merchandise and asking, say, at the shirt counter, about the material, color, style, cuffs, collars, and price. As the group occupying the clerks' attention around the shirt counters moved to the underwear section, those at the underwear section would replace them at the shirt counter, and the personnel of the store would be constantly occupied.

Now pause to examine the tactic. It is legal. There is no sit-in or unlawful occupation of premises. Some thousands of people are in the store "shopping." The police are powerless and you are operating within the law.

This operation would go on until an hour before closing time, when the group would begin purchasing everything in sight to be delivered C.O.D.! This would tie up truck-delivery service for at least two days—with obvious further heavy financial costs, since all the merchandise would be refused at the time of delivery.

The threat was delivered to the authorities through a legitimate and "trustworthy" channel. Every organization must have two or three stool pigeons who are trusted by the establishment. These stool pigeons are invaluable as "trustworthy" lines of communication to the establishment. With all plans ready to go, we began formation of a series of committees: a transportation committee to get the buses, a mobilization committee to work with the ministers to get their people to their buses, and other committees with other specific functions. Two of the key committees deliberately included one of these stoolies each, so that there would be one to back up the other. We knew the plan would be quickly reported back to the department store. The next day we received a call from the department store for a meeting to discuss new personnel policies and an urgent request that the meeting take place within the next two or three days, certainly before Saturday!

The personnel policies of the store were drastically changed. Overnight, 186 new jobs were opened. For the first time, blacks were on the sales floor and in executive training.

This is the kind of tactic that can be used by the middle class too. Organized shopping, wholesale buying plus charging and returning everything on delivery, would add accounting costs to their attack on the retailer with the ominous threat of continued repetition. This is far more effective than canceling a charge account. Let's look at the score: (1) sales for one day are completely shot; (2) delivery service is tied up for two days or more; and (3) the accounting department is screwed up. The total cost is a nightmare for any retailer, and the sword remains hanging over his head. The middle class, too, must learn the nature of the enemy and be able to practice what I have described as mass jujitsu, utilizing the power of one part of the power structure against another part.

COMPETITION

Once we understand the external reactions of the Haves to the challenges of the Have-Nots, then we go to the next level of examination, the anatomy of power of the Haves among themselves.

But let us go deeper into the psyche of this Goliath. The Haves possess and in turn are possessed by power. Obsessed with the fear of losing power, their every move is dictated by the idea of keeping it. The way of life of the Haves is to keep what they have and wherever possible to shore up their defenses.

This opens a new vista—not only do we have a whole class determined to keep its power and in constant conflict with the Have-Nots; at the same time, they are in conflict among themselves. Power is not static; it cannot be frozen and preserved like food; it must grow or die. Therefore, in order to keep power the status quo must get more. But from whom? There is just so much more than can be squeezed out of the Have-Nots—so the Haves must take it from each other. They are on a road from which there is no turning back. This power cannibalism of the Haves permits only temporary truces, and only when equally confronted by a common enemy. Even then there are regular breaks in the ranks, as individual units attempt to exploit the general threat for their own special benefit. Here is the vulnerable belly of the status quo.

I first learned this lesson during the 1930s depression, when the United States experienced a revolutionary upheaval in the form of a mass labor-union-organizing drive known as the C.I.O. This was the radical wing of the labor movement; it espoused industrial unionism while the conservative and archaic A.F. of L. clung to craft unionism. The position of the A.F. of L. excluded the masses of workers from union organization. The battle cry of the C.I.O. was "organize the unorganized." Very quickly the issue was joined with the gargantuan automobile industry,

which was at that time an open shop, and completely
unorganized. The first attack was against the behemoth
of this empire, General Motors. A sit-down strike was
launched against Chevrolet. John L. Lewis, then the leader
of the C.I.O., told me that at the height of this sit-down
strike he heard a rumor that General Motors had met with
both Ford and Chrysler to advance the following proposition: "We at General Motors are fighting your battle for
if the C.I.O. beats us, then you're next in line and there
will be no stopping them. Now we are willing to let the
C.I.O. sit in at Chevrolet until hell freezes and suffer that
loss in our profits *if* you will hold your production of Fords
and Plymouths [the price-class competitors to the Chevro-
let] to your present market. On the other hand, we cannot
hold out against the C.I.O. if you boost production in
order to sell to all potential Chevrolet customers who will
buy your products because they cannot get Chevrolets."

Lewis, who was an organizational genius with a rare
insight into the power mechanics of the status quo, dismissed it with a perceptive comment. It doesn't matter
whether this is a false rumor or true, he said, because
neither Ford nor Chrysler could ever agree to overlook
an opportunity for an immediate increase in their profits
and power, shortsighted as it might be.

The internecine struggle among the Haves for their
individual self-interest is as shortsighted as internecine
struggle among the Have-Nots. I have on occasion re-
marked that I feel confident that I could persuade a mil-
lionaire on a Friday to subsidize a revolution for Saturday
out of which he would make a huge profit on Sunday even
though he was certain to be executed on Monday.

Once one understands this internal battle for power
within the status quo, one can begin to appraise effective

tactics to exploit it. It is sad to see the stupidity of inex-
perienced organizers who make gross errors by failing to
have even an elementary appreciation of this pattern.

An example is to be found just a couple of years ago
when during the height of the rising tide of the struggle
for civil rights certain civil rights leaders in Chicago declared a Christmas boycott on *all* the department stores
downtown. The boycott was a disastrous failure, and any
experienced revolutionary could have predicted without
any reservations that this would have been the case. Any
attack against the status quo must use the strength of the
enemy against itself. Let us examine this particular boycott—the error was in trying to boycott *all*, instead of
some. Few liberals, white or black, would forgo all Christmas shopping in the most attractive shopping places. Even
if it had not been the Christmas season, we know that
picket lines are relatively ineffective today in stopping the
general population. There is a low degree of identification
on the part of the general population with the labor movement or with picket lines in general. However, even that
low degree can be exploited by placing a picket line in
front of only one department store. If the same merchandise can be purchased at the same price at another department store across the street, the slight uneasiness that
the picket line creates can affect a significant number of
customers—they have an easy enough, visible enough alternative: they will cross the street. The power squeeze
comes when the picketed department store sees a number
of customers going across to its competitors.

This calculated maneuvering of the power of one
part of the Haves against its other parts is central to
strategy. In a certain sense it is similar to the Have-Not
nations playing off the U.S.A. against the U.S.S.R.

THEIR OWN PETARD

The basic tactic in warfare against the Haves is a mass
political jujitsu: the Have-Nots do not rigidly oppose the
Haves, but yield in such planned and skilled ways that
the superior strength of the Haves becomes their own
undoing. For example, since the Haves publicly pose as
the custodians of responsibility, morality, law, and justice
(which are frequently strangers to each other), they can
be constantly pushed to live up to their own book of
morality and regulations. No organization, including organized religion, can live up to the letter of its own book.
You can club them to death with their "book" of rules and
regulations. This is what that great revolutionary, Paul of
Tarsus, knew when he wrote to the Corinthians: "Who
also hath made us able ministers of the New Testament;
not of the letter, but of the spirit; for the letter killeth."

Let us take, for example, the case of the civil rights
demonstrations of 1963 in Birmingham, when thousands
of Negro children stayed out of school to participate in
the street demonstrations. The Birmingham Board of Education dusted off its book of regulations and threatened to
expel all children absent for this reason. Here the civil
rights leaders erred (as they did on other vital tactics)
by backing off instead of rushing in with more demonstrations and pressing the Birmingham Board of Education
between the pages of their book of regulations by forcing
them to live up to the letter of their regulations and statements. The Board and the City of Birmingham would have
been in an impossible situation with every Negro child

expelled and loose on the streets—if they didn't reverse themselves before they acted, they would have reversed themselves one day later.

Another dramatic failure to understand tactics came during the second Chicago public school boycott, in 1964, a struggle against a de facto segregated public school system. We know that the efficacy of any action is in the reaction it evokes from the Haves, so that the cycle escalates in a continuum of conflict. Lacking any reaction from the Haves (except public notice of the numbers of children involved), effects of the boycott were significantly over by the next day. This boycott was what I call a terminal tactic, one that crests, breaks, and disappears like a wave. Terminal tactics do not arouse the reaction that is essential for the development of a conflict. A terminal tactic is to be exercised only to finish a conflict, for it is ineffective in the development of the rhythm of give and take that one must have while stepping up the war and building the movement.

Civil rights leaders could console themselves with the "psychological carry-overs," "public display of support," and similar prayerful hopes, but as for carrying on the conflict for integration, that was over and done with by the next day. Nice memory.

In Chicago the Haves slipped badly when both a judge and a district attorney muttered that the book of regulations banned attempts to induce the absence of public school students, and growled ominously about an injunction against all civil rights leaders taking part in the development of the boycott. Here, as always, whenever the Haves start living by their book they present a golden opportunity to the Have-Nots to transform what had been a terminal tactic into a sweeping advance on

many fronts. The children wouldn't need to be absent—
the leaders would be the only people who needed to act.
Now was the time to start an intensive campaign of ridicule, insults, and taunting defiance, daring the district
attorney and the judge either to live up to their regulations
and issue the injunctions or stand publicly exposed as
fearful frauds who were afraid to put the law where their
mouths were. Such behavior on the part of the Have-Nots
would probably have resulted in the injunction. But by
this time the boycott tactic would have had shaking consequences. Immediately following the boycott every civil
rights leader in the city of Chicago involved in it would
have been in violation of the court injunction. But the
last thing that the establishment wants is to indict and
imprison every single civil rights leader (which would
have included leaders of every religious organization in
town) in the city of Chicago. Such a step would have
shaken the power structure of Chicago, and certainly put
the entire issue of school segregation policy on the line.
Without any question, the district attorney and the judge
would have had to depend on postponements in the hope
that everybody would just forget about it. At this point,
now that the civil rights leaders had the powerful weapon
of the book of laws of the Haves, they would have to
stand fast publicly—once again taunting, insulting, demanding that the judge and the district attorney "obey
the law," charging that the district attorney and the courts
had issued an injunction which they had publicly, will-
fully, and maliciously violated, and that they therefore
must be compelled to pay the penalties for this action.
If the civil rights leaders insisted that they be arrested and
tried, the Haves would be on the run and in complete
confusion, caught in the strait jacket of their own book.

Enforcement of their injunction would have resulted in a citywide storm of protest and a rapid growth in the organization. Non-enforcement would have signaled a breakdown and retreat of the Haves from the Have-Nots, and also resulted in swelling the size and force of the Have-Not organization.

TIME IN JAIL

The reaction of the status quo in jailing revolutionary leaders is in itself a tremendous contribution to the development of the Have-Not movement as well as to the personal development of the revolutionary leaders. This point should be carefully remembered as another example of how mass jujitsu tactics can be used to so maneuver the status quo that it turns its power against itself.

Jailing the revolutionary leaders and their followers performs three vital functions for the cause of the Have-Nots: (1) it is an act on the part of the status quo that in itself points up the conflict between the Haves and the Have-Nots; (2) it strengthens immeasurably the position of the revolutionary leaders with their people by surrounding the jailed leadership with an aura of martyrdom; (3) it deepens the identification of the leadership with their people since the prevalent reaction among the Have-Nots is that their leadership cares so much for them, and is so sincerely committed to the issue, that it is willing to suffer imprisonment for the cause. Repeatedly in situations where the relationship between the Have-Nots and their leaders has become strained the remedy has been the jailing of the leaders by the establishment. Immediately the ranks close and the leaders regain their mass support.

At the same time, the revolutionary leaders should make certain that their publicized violations of the regulations are so selected that their jail terms are relatively brief, from one day to two months. The trouble with a long jail sentence is that (a) a revolutionary is removed from action for such an extended period of time that he loses touch, and (b) if you are gone long enough everybody forgets about you. Life goes on, new issues arise, and new leaders appear; however, a periodic removal from circulation by being jailed is an essential element in the development of the revolutionary. The one problem that the revolutionary cannot cope with by himself is that he must now and then have an opportunity to reflect and synthesize his thoughts. To gain that privacy in which he can try to make sense out of what he is doing, why he is doing it, where he is going, what has been wrong with what he has done, what he should have done and above all to see the relationships of all the episodes and acts as they tie in to a general pattern, the most convenient and accessible solution is jail. It is here that he begins to develop a philosophy. It is here that he begins to shape long-term goals, intermediate goals, and a self-analysis of tactics as tied to his own personality. It is here that he is emancipated from the slavery of action wherein he was compelled to think from act to act. Now he can look at the totality of his actions and the reactions of the enemy from a fairly detached position.

Every revolutionary leader of consequence has had to undergo these withdrawals from the arena of action. Without such opportunities, he goes from one tactic and one action to another, but most of them are almost terminal

tactics in themselves; he never has a chance to think
through an overall synthesis, and he burns himself out. He
becomes, in fact, nothing more than a temporary irritant.
The prophets of the Old Testament and the New found
their opportunity for synthesis by voluntarily removing
themselves to the wilderness. It was after they emerged
that they began propagandizing their philosophies. Often
a revolutionary finds that he cannot voluntarily detach
himself, since the pressure of events and action do not
permit him that luxury; furthermore, a revolutionary or a
man of action does not have the sedentary frame of mind
that is part of the personality of a research scholar. He
finds it very difficult to sit quietly and think and write.
Even when provided with a voluntary situation of that
kind he will react by trying to escape the job of thinking
and writing. He will do anything to avoid it.

I remember that once I accepted an invitation to participate in a one-week discussion at the Aspen Institute.
The argument was made that this would be a good opportunity to get away from it all and write. The institute
sessions would last only from 10:00 to noon and I would
be free for the rest of the afternoon and the evening. The
morning began with the institute sessions; the subjects
were very interesting and carried over through a luncheon
discussion, which lasted until 2:30 or 3:00. Now I could
sit and write from 3:00 to dinner, but then one of the members of the discussion group, a most interesting astronomer,
stopped in for a chat. By the time he left it was 5:00 P.M.;
there wasn't much point in starting to write then, for there
would be cocktails at 5:30, and after cocktails there wasn't
much point in sitting down to start writing because dinner
would be served soon, and after dinner there wasn't much
point in trying to start writing because it was late and I

was tired. Now it is true that I could have got up immediately after lunch, told everybody that I was not to be disturbed, and gone to spend the afternoon writing. I could have gone back to my quarters, locked the door, and, hopefully, started writing; but the fact is that I did not want to come to grips with thinking and writing any more than anyone else involved in revolutionary movements does. I welcomed the interruptions and used them as rationalizing excuses to escape the ordeal of thinking and writing.

Jail provides just the opposite circumstances. You have no phones and, except for an hour or so a day, no visitors. Your jailers are rough, unsociable, and generally so dull that you wouldn't want to talk to them anyway. You find yourself in a physical drabness and confinement, which you desperately try to escape. Since there is no physical escape you are driven to erase your surroundings imaginatively: you escape into thinking and writing. It was through periodic imprisonment that the basis for my first publication and the first orderly philosophical arrangement of my ideas and goals occurred.

TIME IN TACTICS

Enough of philosophical cells—let's get back to the business of the active essentials of organizing. Among the essentials is timing.

Timing is to tactics what it is to everything in life— the difference between success and failure. I don't mean the timing of the start of a tactic—that is important certainly, but as has been stated repeatedly, life does not usually afford the tactician the luxury of time or place when the conflict is engaged. Life does permit, however, that the skilled tactician be conscious of the utilization of time in the use of tactics.

Once the battle is joined and a tactic is employed, it is important that the conflict not be carried on over too long a time. If you will recall, this was the seventh rule noted at the beginning of this chapter. There are many reasons of human experience arguing for this point. I cannot repeat too often that *a conflict that drags on too long becomes a drag*. The same universality applies for a tactic or for any other specific action.

Among the reasons is the simple fact that human beings can sustain an interest in a particular subject only over a limited period of time. The concentration, the emotional fervor, even the physical energy, a particular experience that is exciting, challenging, and inviting, can last just so long—this is true of the gamut of human behavior, from sex to conflict. After a period of time it becomes monotonous, repetitive, an emotional treadmill, and worse than anything else a bore. From the moment the tactician engages in conflict, his enemy is time.

This should be kept in mind when one is considering boycotts. First, any consideration of a boycott should carefully avoid essentials such as meat, milk, bread, or basic vegetables, since even selective buying weakens after a period of time as the opponent cuts his prices below his competitors. With non-essentials—grapes, bananas, pistachio nuts, maraschino cherries, and the like—many liberals can make the "sacrifice" and feel noble.

Even so, any skilled organizer knows that he can push this negative over into a positive: he can compel or maneuver the opposition to make the mistake themselves. The drama of continuous involvement builds up an immunity to any further excitement. The consequence is that the opposition will finally, out of their own tedium, give in.

The pressure of time should be ever-present in the mind of the tactician as he begins to engage in action. This applies to the physical action such as a mass demonstration as well as to its emotional counterpart. When the Woodlawn Organization in Chicago decided to have a massive move-in on City Hall with reference to an issue on education, 5,000 to 8,000 individuals were to fill the lobby of City Hall in Chicago at 10:00 A.M. for a confrontation with the mayor. At the time the strategy was being developed, the function of time in the use of the tactic was examined and understood, and therefore the tactic was utilized to its fullest potential rather than turning into a debacle, as was the case with the recent poor people's march, Resurrection City, etc. There was a clear understanding on the part of the leadership that when some thousands of people are assembled downtown, the physical tedium of standing, of being in one place for a period of time, begins to dampen ardor rather soon, and that small groups will begin to disappear to go shopping, go sight-seeing, get refreshments. In short, the life of the immediate metropolitan area becomes much more attractive and inviting than simply being in City Hall in an action that has already spent the excitement of witnessing the opposition's shock. After a while—and by "a while" meaning two to three hours—the 8,000 would have dwindled to 800 or less and the impact of mass numbers would have been seriously diluted and weakened. Furthermore, the effect on the opposition would have been that the mayor, seeing a mass action of 8,000 shrink to 800, would assume that if he only sits it out for another two or three hours the 800 will shrink to 80, and if he sits it out for a day there will be nothing left. That would have gained us nothing.

With this in mind, the leadership of the Woodlawn Organization made its confrontation with the mayor, told the mayor that they wanted action and quickly on their particular demands, and that they were going to give him just so much time to meet their demands. Having given their message, they said, they were now calling off their demonstration, but they would be back in the same numbers or more. And with that they turned around and led their still-enthusiastic army in an organized, fully armed, powerful withdrawal, and left this mass impression upon the City Hall authorities.

There is a way to keep the action going and to prevent it from being a drag, but this means constantly cutting new issues as the action continues, so that by the time the enthusiasm and the emotions for one issue have started to de-escalate, a new issue has come into the scene with a consequent revival. With a constant introduction of new issues, it will go on and on. This is the case with many prolonged fights; in the end, the negotiations don't even involve the issues around which the conflict originally began. It brings to mind the old anecdote of the Hundred Years' War in Europe: when the parties finally got together for peace negotiations nobody could remember what the war was all about, or how it had begun—and furthermore, whatever the original issues, they were now irrelevant to the peace negotiations.

NEW TACTICS AND OLD

Speaking of issues, let's look at the issue of pollution. Here again, we can use the Haves against the Haves to get what we want. When utilities or heavy industries talk about the "people," they mean the banks and other power sectors of their own world. If their banks, say, start pressing them, then they listen and hurt. The target, therefore, should be the banks that serve the steel, auto, and other industries, and the goal, significant lessening of pollution.

Let us begin by making the banks live up to their own public statements.

All banks want money and advertise for new savings and checking accounts. They even offer premium prizes to those who will open accounts. Opening a savings account in a bank is more than a routine matter. First, you sit down with one of the multiple vice-presidents or employees and begin to fill out forms and respond to questions for at least thirty minutes. If a thousand or more people all moved in, each with $5 or $10 to open up a savings account, the bank's floor functions would be paralyzed. Again, as in the case of the shop-in, the police would be immobilized. There is no illegal occupation. The bank is in a difficult position. It knows what is happening, but still it does not want to antagonize would-be depositors. The bank's public image would be destroyed if some thousand would-be depositors were arrested or forcibly ejected from the premises.

The element of ridicule is here again. A continuous chain of action and reaction is formed. Following this, the people can return in a few days and close their accounts, and then return again later to open new accounts. This is what I would call a middle-class guerrilla attack. It could well cause an irrational reaction on the part of the banks which could then be directed against their large customers, for example the polluting utilities or whatever were the obvious, stated targets of the middle-class organizations. The target of a secondary attack such as this is always outraged; the bank, thus, is likely to react more emotionally since it as a body feels that it is innocent, being punished for another's sins.

At the same time, this kind of action can also be combined with social refreshments and gathering together with friends downtown, as well as with the general enjoyment of seeing the discomfiture and confusion on the part of the establishment. The middle-class guerrillas would enjoy themselves as they increased the pressure on their enemies.

Once a specific tactic is used, it ceases to be outside the experience of the enemy. Before long he devises countermeasures that void the previous effective tactic. Recently the head of a corporation showed me the blueprint of a new plant and pointed to a large ground-floor area: "Boy, have we got an architect who is with it!" he chuckled. "See that big hall? That's our sit-in room! When the sit-inners come they'll be shown in and there will be coffee, T.V., and good toilet facilities—they can sit here until hell freezes over."

Now you can relegate sit-ins to the Smithsonian Museum.

Once, though—and in rare circumstances even now—sit-downs were really revolutionary. A vivid illustration was the almost spontaneous sit-down strikes of the United

Automobile Workers Union in their 1937 organizing drive at General Motors. The seizure of private property caused an uproar in the nation. With rare exception every labor leader ran for cover—this was too revolutionary for them. The sit-down strikers began to worry about the illegality of their action and the why and wherefore, and it was then that the chief of all C.I.O. organizers, Lewis, gave them their rationale. He thundered, "The right to a man's job transcends the right of private property! The C.I.O. stands squarely behind these sit-downs!"

The sit-down strikers at G.M. cheered. _Now_ they knew _why_ they had done what they did, and _why_ they would stay to the end. The lesson here is that a major job of the organizer is to instantly develop the rationale for actions which have taken place by accident or impulsive anger. Lacking the rationale, the action becomes inexplicable to its participants and rapidly disintegrates into defeat. Possessing a rationale gives action a meaning and purpose.

The Genesis of
Tactic Proxy

THE GREATEST BARRIER to communication between myself and would-be organizers arises when I try to get across the concept that tactics are not the product of careful cold reason, that they do not follow a table of organization or plan of attack. Accident, unpredictable reactions to your own actions, necessity, and improvisation dictate the direction and nature of tactics. Then, analytical logic is required to appraise where you are, what you can do next, the risks and hopes that you can look forward to. It is this analysis that protects you from being a blind prisoner of the tactic and the accidents that accompany it. But I cannot overemphasize that the tactic itself comes out of the free flow of action and reaction, and requires on the part of the organizer an easy acceptance of apparent disorganization.

The organizer goes with the action. His approach must be free, open-ended, curious, sensitive to any opportunities, any handles to grab on to, even though they involve other issues than those he may have in mind at that particular time. The organizer should never feel lost because he has no plot, no timetable or definite points of reference. A great pragmatist, Abraham Lincoln, told his secretary in the month the war began:

"My policy is to have no policy."

Three years later, in a letter to a Kentucky friend, he confessed plainly: "I have been controlled by events."

The major problem in trying to communicate this idea is that it is outside the experience of practically everyone who has been exposed to our alleged education system. The products of this system have been trained to emphasize order, logic, rational thought, direction, and purpose. We call it mental discipline and it results in a structured, static, closed, rigid, mental makeup. Even a phrase such as "being open-minded" becomes just a verbalism. Happenings that cannot be understood at the time, or don't fit into the accumulated "educational" pattern, are considered strange, suspect, and to be avoided. For anyone to understand what anyone else is doing, he has got to understand it in terms of logic, rational decision, and deliberate conscious action. Therefore when you try to communicate the whys and wherefores of your actions you are compelled to fabricate these logical, rational, structured reasons to rationalizations. This is not how it is in real life.

Since the nature of the development of tactics cannot be described as a general proposition, I shall attempt instead to present a case study of the development of the proxy tactic, one that promises to be a major tactic for some years to come. I shall try to take the reader into *my* experience with the hope that afterward he will reflect candidly upon the hows and whys of his own tactical experience.

We know that we are predominantly a middle-class society living in a corporate economy, an economy that tends to form conglomerates so that in order to know where the power lies, you have to find out who owns whom. For some years past it's been like trying to find the pea in the shell game—but now there are strobe lights flashing for further confusion. The one thing certain is that masses of middle-class Americans are ready to move toward major confrontations with corporate America.

College students have argued that their administrations should give student committees the proxies in their stock portfolios for use in the struggle for peace and against pollution, inflation, racially discriminatory policies, and other evils.

Citizens from Baltimore to Los Angeles are organizing proxy groups to pool their votes for action on the social and political policies of "their" corporations. Feeling that national proxy organization may give them, for the first time, the power to do something, they are now waking to a growing interest in the relationship of their corporate holdings to the Pentagon.

This pragmatic means toward political action has loosed new forces. Recently I talked to three students at Stanford's School of Business Administration about the ways and means of proxy use. I asked them what their major goal was and they responded, "Getting out of Vietnam." They shook their heads when I asked whether they had been active on this issue. "Why not?" I inquired. Their answer was that they didn't believe in the effectiveness of demonstrations in the streets, and recoiled from such actions as carrying Viet Cong flags, draft card burning or draft evasion, but they did believe in the use of proxies. Enter three new recruits; you can depend upon the establishment to radicalize them further.

Like any new political program, the proxy tactic was

not the result of reason and logic—it was part accident, part necessity, part response to reaction, and part imagination, and each part affected the other. Of course "imagination" is also tactical sensitivity; when the "accident" happens, the imaginative organizer recognizes it and grabs it before it slips by.

The various accounts of the "history" of the development of the proxy tactic show a line of reason, purpose, and order that were never there. The mythology of "history" is usually so pleasant for the ego of the subject that he accepts it in a "modest" silence, an affirmation of the validity of the mythology. After a while he begins to believe it.

The further danger of mythology is that it carries the picture of "genius at work" with the false implication of purposeful logic and planned actions. This makes it more difficult to free oneself from the structured approach. For this if no other reason mythology should be understood for what it is.

The history of Chicago's Back of the Yards Council reads, "Out from the gutters, the bars, the churches, the labor unions, yes, even the communist and socialist parties; the neighborhood businessmen's associations, the American Legion and Chicago's Catholic Bishop Bernard Sheil. They all came together on July 14, 1939. July 14, Bastille Day! Their Bastille Day, the day they deliberately and symbolically selected to join together to storm the barricades of unemployment, rotten housing, disease, delinquency and demoralization."

That's the way it reads. What really happened is that July 14 was selected because it was the one day the public park fieldhouse was clear—the one day that the labor unions had no scheduled meetings—the day that many priests thought was best—the one day that the late Bishop

Sheil was free. There wasn't a thought of Bastille Day in any of our minds.

That day at a press conference before the convention came to order a reporter asked me, "Don't you think it's somewhat too revolutionary to deliberately select Bastille Day for your first convention?" I tried to cover my surprise but I thought, "How wonderful! What a windfall!" I answered, "Not at all. It is fitting that we do so and that's why we did it."

I quickly informed all the speakers about "Bastille Day" and it became the keynote of nearly every speech. And so history records it as a "calculated, planned" tactic.

The difference between fact and history was brought home when I was a visiting professor at a certain Eastern university. Two candidates there were taking their written examinations for the doctorate in community organization and criminology. I persuaded the president of this college to get me a copy of this examination and when I answered the questions the departmental head graded my paper, knowing only that I was an anonymous friend of the president. Three of the questions were on the philosophy and motivations of Saul Alinsky. I answered two of them incorrectly. I did not know what my philosophy or motivations were; but they did!

I remember that when I organized the Back of the Yards in Chicago I made many moves almost intuitively. But when I was asked to explain what I had done and why, I had to come up with *reasons*. Reasons that were not present at the time. What I did at the time, I did because that was the thing to do; it was the best thing to do, or it was the only thing to do. However, when pressed for reasons I had to start considering an intellectual scaffolding for my past actions—really, rationalizations. I can remember the "reasons" being so convincing even to myself that I thought, "Why, of course, I did it for those reasons—I should have known that that was why I did it."

The proxy tactic was born in Rochester, New York, in the conflict between Eastman Kodak and the black ghetto organization called FIGHT our foundation had helped to organize. The issues* of the conflict are not relevant to the present subject except that a vice-president of Kodak assigned to negotiate with FIGHT reached an agreement with FIGHT, and that seemed to close the matter. Enter the first accident, for Kodak then repudiated its own vice-president and the agreement he had made. This re-opened the battle. If Kodak had not reneged, the issue would have ended there.

Now necessity moved in. As the lines were drawn for battle it became clear that the usual strategy of demonstrations and confrontations would be unavailing. While Kodak's buildings and administration were in Rochester, its real life was throughout its American and overseas markets. Demonstrations might be embarrassing and inconvenient, but they would not be the tactic to force an agreement. It wasn't Rochester that Eastman Kodak was concerned about. Their image in that community could

---

* Those involved in the Kodak-FIGHT battle knew that there was one issue—"Would Kodak or any other corporation recognize FIGHT as the bargaining agent for the black ghetto of Rochester, New York?" Once Kodak recognized FIGHT as representing the black ghetto, we could come to the table to negotiate on all other issues, including the employment of more blacks. Kodak's recognition of FIGHT would result in other corporations following suit and this would lead to other programs and other issues. Kodak's subsequent recognition of FIGHT caused Xerox to do the same and resulted in the launching of a black-owned and black-manned factory by FIGHT called FIGHTON in collaboration with the Xerox Corporation.

always be sustained by sheer financial power. Their vulnerability was throughout the nation and overseas.

We then began looking for appropriate tactics. An economic boycott was rejected because of Kodak's overwhelming domination of the film-negative market. Thus a call for an economic boycott would be asking the American people to stop taking pictures, which obviously would not work as long as babies were being born, children were graduating, having birthday parties, getting married, going on picnics and so forth. The idea of boycott did evoke thoughts of checking out the Sherman Anti-Trust Act against them at some point. Other wild ideas were tossed about.°

° *The National Observer,* July 17, 1967: "Civil-rights activists have devised a major new plan to bring pressure on some of the nation's biggest corporations, The National Observer learned last week. These activists plan to wage proxy battles—hoping to push management into providing more jobs for poor whites and Negroes. . . .

"The Eastman Kodak case was the guidepost. It was not until the late-blooming proxy battle that Rochester's FIGHT made headway. Before the proxy fight, there were few ways in which pressure could be brought on the dominant international photography company.

" 'Eastman Kodak wasn't worried about what FIGHT could do, and I don't blame them,' Mr. Alinsky says. 'A boycott was out of the question. That would be like asking everyone to stop taking pictures. This called for a new kind of tactic, and we hit on one.

" 'We had all kinds of plans. We had heard that Queen Elizabeth owned Kodak stock. So we were considering throwing up a picket line around Buckingham Palace in London, and charging that the changing of the guard was a conspiracy to encourage picture-taking. But we didn't have time to follow this or a lot of other things up. If we have time to plan a campaign, it could be much more effective.'

"The thought of the Buckingham Palace picket line may seem ludicrous, but it is typical of Alinsky methods—attention-getting and outrageous to the point of amusement. His basic philosophy, as he has often stated, is that the poor, who lack the money or authority to challenge the 'power structure,' must use the only weapon they have at their command—people and publicity."

The proxy idea first came up as a way to gain entrance to the annual stockholders' meeting for harassment and publicity, and again accident and necessity played a part. I had recently accepted a number of invitations to address universities, religious conventions, and similar organizations in various parts of the United States. Why not talk to them about the Kodak-FIGHT battle and ask for proxies? Why not accept all speaking invitations even if it meant ninety consecutive days in ninety different places? It wouldn't cost us a penny. These places not only paid fees to my organization, but they also paid travel expenses.

And so it began with nothing specific in mind except to ask Eastman Kodak stockholders to assign their proxies to the Rochester black organization or come to the stockholders' meeting and vote in favor of FIGHT.

There was never any thought, then or now, of using proxies to gain economic power inside the corporation or to elect directors to the board. I couldn't be less interested in having a couple of directors elected to the board of Kodak or any other corporation. As long as the opposition has the majority, that's it. Also, boards of directors are only rubber stamps of management. With the exception of some management people "retired" to the board, the rest of them don't know which way is up.

The first real breakthrough followed my address to the National Unitarian Convention in Denver on May 3, 1967, in which I asked for and received the passage of a resolution that the proxies of their organization would be given to FIGHT. The reactions of the local politicians made me realize that senators and congressmen up for reelection would turn to their research directors and ask, "How many Unitarians have I got in my district?" Th proxy tactic now began to look like a possible political bank-shot. Political leaders who saw their churches assigning proxies to us could see them assigning their votes as well. This meant political power. Kodak has money, but money counts in elections for television time, newspaper ads, political workers, publicity, pay-offs and pressure. If this fails to get the vote, money is politically useless. It was obvious that politicians who would support us had everything to gain.

Proxies were now seen as proof of political intent if they came from large membership organizations. The church organizations had mass members—*voters!* It meant publicity and publicity meant pressure on political candidates and incumbents. We hoisted a banner with our slogan, "Keep your sermons; give us your proxies," and set sail into the sea of churches. I couldn't help noting the irony that churches, having sold their spiritual birthright in exchange for donations of stock, could now go straight again by giving their proxies to the poor.

The pressure began to build. My only concern was whether Kodak would get the message. Never before or since have I encountered an American corporation so politically insensitive. I wondered whether Kodak would have to be brought before a Senate subcommittee hearing before it would wake up and give in. The building of political support would have prepared the ground for two actions: (1) a Senate subcommittee hearing in which a number of practices would be exposed and (2) the possibility of an investigation by the Attorney-General's office. Kodak would reconsider dealing with us if those two were the alternatives. I had an understanding with the late Senator Robert Kennedy to advise him when we were ready to move. In my discussions with Kennedy, I found

that his commitment was not political but human. He was
outraged by the conditions in the Rochester ghetto.

I began looking over the national scene for avenues of
attack. Foundations such as Ford, Rockefeller, Carnegie,
and others with substantial investments, were ostensibly
committed to social progress. So were union retirement
funds. I planned to ask them, "If you are on the level, then
prove it at no cost to yourselves. We are not asking for a
penny. Just assign us the proxies of the stock you hold."
The effect of foundation proxies would, of course, be
marginal since their proxies, unlike those of the churches,
represented no constituencies. Even so, they were not to
be dismissed.

Other ideas began to occur. This was a whole new ball
game for me and my curiosity sent me scurrying and
sniffing at the many opportunities in this great Wall Street
Wonderland. I didn't know where I was going, but that
was part of the fascination. I wasn't the least worried. I
knew that accident or necessity or both would tell us,
"Hey, we go this way." Since I didn't seem disturbed or
confused everyone believed I had a secret and totally
organized Machiavellian campaign. No one suspected the
truth. The *Los Angeles Times* said:

> . . . the Kodak proxy battle created waves
> throughout the corporate world. Heads of several
> large corporations and representatives of some
> mutual funds have tried to contact Alinsky to fer-
> ret out the rest of his plans. One corporation ex-
> ecutive told a reporter, "When I asked him what
> he was going to do next he said he did not know.
> I do not believe that."
>
> A reporter asked Alinsky what he is going to
> do next with the proxies. "I honestly do not know,"

he said. "Sure, I have plans, but you know that a thing like this opens up its own possibilities, things you never thought of. Man, we can have a ball, a real ball!"

This was all virgin territory. In the past a few individuals had gone to stockholders' meetings to sound off, but at best they were minor irritants. No one had ever organized a campaign to use proxies for social and political purposes.

The good old establishment made its usual contribution. Corporation executives sought me out. Their anxious questions convinced me that we had the razor to cut through the golden curtain that protected the so-called private sector from facing its public responsibilities. Business publications added their violent attacks and convinced me further.° In all my wars with the establishment I had never seen it so uptight. I knew there was dynamite in the proxy scare. But where? "Where" meant "how."

As I meandered around this jungle, looking for some kind of a power pattern, I began to notice things. Look! DuPont owns a nice piece of Kodak, and so does this and that corporation. And those mutual funds! They've got more than $60 billion in stock investments and their hold-

---

° *Barron's* National Business and Financial Weekly, May 1, 1967, "Who's Out of Focus?": ". . . Perhaps the most memorable event of the season occurred at Flemington, N.J., where Eastman Kodak Co. held its annual meeting on Tuesday . . . Perhaps by coincidence, in a generally strong market Eastman Kodak stock promptly dropped half-a-dozen points . . . Companies best serve their stockholders and communities by sticking to business . . . [Alinsky was described] by 'Muhammad Speaks,' house organ of the Black Muslims, as 'one of the world's great sociologists and criminologists'. . . For Kodak and the rest of U.S. industry, it's time to stop turning the other cheek . . . management is the steward of other people's property. It can never afford to forget where its primary obligations lie."

ings include Kodak. After all, mutual funds have annual meetings and proxies too. Suppose we had proxies in every corporation in America and suppose we were fighting Corporation X and suppose we also had proxies for the various corporations that had stock in Corporation X and proxies for other corporations that had stock in the corporations that had stock in Corporation X.

Soon I was intoxicated by the possibilities. You could begin to play the whole Wall Street Board up and down. You could go to, say, Corporation Z, point out your proxy holding there, mention that there were certain grievances you had against them for some of their bad policy operations, but that you were willing to forget about them (for the time being) if they would use their stock to put pressure on Corporation Q for the sake of influencing Corporation X. The same muscle could be applied to Corporation Q itself. You could make your deals up and down. Always operating in your favor was the self-interest of the corporations and the fact that they hate each other. This is what I would call corporate jujitsu.

Recently I was at a luncheon meeting with a number of presidents of major corporations where one of them expressed his fear that I saw things only in terms of power rather than from the point of view of good will and reason. I replied that when he and his corporation approached other corporations in terms of reason, good will, and cooperation, instead of going for the jugular, that would be the day that I would be happy to pursue the conversation. The subject was dropped.

Proxies represented a key to participation by the middle class. But the question was how to organize it. Imagination had had its moment. It was time for accident or necessity or both to come on stage. I found myself saying, "Accident, accident, where the hell are you?"

Then it came! The *Los Angeles Times* carried a front-page story on the proxy tactic. Soon we were deluged with mail, including sackfuls of proxies of different corporations. One letter read, "I have $10,000 to invest. What kind of stock should I buy? What kind of proxies do you need? Should I buy Dow Chemical?" But the two most important letters provided the *accident* that pointed to the next step. "Enclosed find my proxies. I wonder whether you have heard from anyone else in my suburb? If you have, I would appreciate receiving their names and addresses so that I can call a housemeeting and organize a San Fernando Valley Chapter of Proxies for People." The second letter said, "I'm all for it but I don't know why you should have the right to decide which corporations should be attacked—after all, they are our proxies and we would like to have something to say about it. *Also, we don't know why you should go to the board meetings with our proxies —why can't we go with our proxies, of course all organized and knowing what we want, but we would like to go ourselves.*"*

It was these two letters that kicked open the door. Of course! For years I had been saying power is with people! How stupid could I be? There it was! Instead of annual put-ons like Eastman Kodak's in Flemington, New Jersey, where the company buses down a dozen loads of stock-holding payrollers to a public school auditorium—for a day off with pay and a free lunch (and a crumby one at that) they sing out their Sieg Heils and back to Rochester--

---

* Emphasis added.

let's make them hold their meetings in Newark or Jersey City in the ball park, or outdoors in Atlantic City, where thousands and thousands of proxy holders can attend. Yankee Stadium in New York or Soldier Field in Chicago would be better, but many of America's corporations are incorporated in special protective sanctuaries like New Jersey or Delaware and would claim that they must meet in these states. Well, President Nixon has set up the precedent for sanctuaries. Let's see what happens when Flemington, New Jersey, with its one beat-up hotel and two motels, faces an invasion of 50,000 stockholders. Will the state call out the National Guard to keep stockholders out of their annual meeting? Remember these are not hippies but American citizens in the most establishment sense—stockholders! What could be more American than that?

Let's imagine a situation in which 75,000 people vote "no" and one man says, "On behalf of the majority of the proxies assigned to management I vote 'aye' and the ayes have it." I would dare management to expose themselves in this way.

But the real importance of those letters was that they showed a way for the middle class to organize. These people, the vast majority of Americans, who feel helpless in the huge corporate economy, who don't know which way to turn, have begun to turn *away* from America, to abdicate as citizens. They rationalize their action by saying that, after all, the experts and the government will take care of it all. They are like the Have-Nots who, when unorganized and powerless, simply resign themselves to a sad scene. Proxies can be the mechanism by which these people can organize, and once they are organized they will re-enter the life of politics. Once organized around proxies they will have a reason to examine, to become educated about, the various corporation policies and practices both domestic and foreign—because now they can do something about them.

There will even be "fringe benefits." Trips to stockholders' meetings will bring drama and adventure into otherwise colorless and sedentary suburban lives. Proxy organizations will help bridge the generation gap, as parents and children join in the battle against the Pentagon and the corporations.

Proxies can be the effective path to the Pentagon. The late General Douglas MacArthur in his farewell speech to the Congress uttered a half truth; "Old generals never die, they just fade away." General MacArthur should have completed his statement by saying "they fade away to Lockheed, Boeing, General Dynamics, and other corporations." Two years before retirement a general will be found already scouting and setting up his "fade-away" corporation sanctuary.

One can envisage the scene where a general informs a corporate executive that a $50 million order will be coming to the corporation for the making of nerve gas, napalm, defoliants, or any other of the great products we export for the benefit of mankind. Instead of a reaction of gratitude and a "General, as soon as you retire we would like to talk to you about your future," he encounters a "Well, look, General, I appreciate your considering us for this contract but we've got a stockholders' meeting coming up next month and the hell that would blow when these thousands of stockholders heard about it—well, General, I don't want to think about it. And we certainly couldn't keep it quiet. It's been very nice seeing you."

Now what has happened? First of all the general has

suddenly realized that corporations are backing away
from the whole war scene. Secondly, the fact that thousands of stockholders would be opposed to this becomes
translated to him as thousands of American citizens, not
long-hairs, not trouble-makers, not Reds, but 200 per cent
bonafide Americans. One could begin to communicate
with the unique (alleged) mentality of the Pentagon
species.

What will be required is a computerized operation
that will quickly give (1) a breakdown of the holdings
of any corporation, (2) a breakdown of holdings of other
corporations that own shares in the target corporation,
and (3) a breakdown of individual stock proxies in the
target corporation and in the corporations that have holdings in the target corporation. It will be necessary to keep
the records of individuals' proxies confidential to protect
people who would rather not let their neighbors know
how many stocks they own.

There will be a nationwide organization, set up either
by myself or others, with national headquarters in Chicago
or New York City, or both. The New York office could
handle all of the computerized operations; the Chicago
office would serve as headquarters for a staff of organizers
who would be constantly on the move through the various
communities of America, from the San Fernando Valley
to Baltimore, and all places in between. Responding to the
interests and requests of local suburban groups, they
would be using their skills to set up organization meetings
and to train volunteer organizers to carry on. The staff
organizers would approach each scene with only one thing
in mind—to get a mass-based middle-class organization
started. The proxy tactic will be common to all these
groups, and each group will gather in any other issues

around which people will organize. They may start by setting up study groups on corporate policies; making recommendations as to the corporations which should be "communicated with" and electing one of theirs as a representative to a national board. The national board will be responsible for the decisions as to corporate targets, issues and policies. The various representatives on the national board will also be responsible for recruiting members of their own local organizations for attendance at annual stockholders' meetings. On this national board will also be representatives of all kinds of consumer organizations as well as churches and other institutions committed to this program. They will be able to contribute invaluable technical advice as well as the support of their own membership.

Remember that the objective of the proxies approach is not simply a power instrument with reference to our corporate economy, but a mechanism providing for a blast-off for middle-class organization—beginning with the proxy, it will then begin to ignite other rockets on the whole political scene from local elections to the congress. Once a people are organized they will keep moving from issue to issue. *People power is the real objective; the proxies are simply a means to that end.*

This total operation will require special fund-raising for the budget essential to the operation. There are many who are already volunteering time and money, but the fund-raising will be difficult since it is obvious that there will be no contributions from corporations or foundations —also, none of the contributions would be tax deductible.

Unquestionably corporations will fight back by pointing out to stockholders that prevention programs on pollution, the rejection of war contracts, or other demands of the stockholders will result in diminished dividends. By the time this occurs, the stockholders will find such satisfaction and meaningfulness in their campaigns that these will be more important than a cut in dividends.

Corporations will change their contributions of stocks to universities. Already it is said that the University of Rochester's Kodak stock cannot be voted by the university, that the voting power is retained by Kodak management —and this presents an interesting legal question. These are some of the potentials and problems of the proxy operation on the American scene. It can mark the beginning of a whole new kind of campaign on campuses against university administrations through their stockholdings. On May 12, 1970, the Stanford University trustees voted their 24,000 shares of General Motors stock in favor of management, in disregard of Stanford's student proposals to use the stock proxies against management. The same at the University of California with 100,000 shares, the University of Michigan with 29,000 shares, the University of Texas for 66,000 shares, Harvard with 287,000 shares, and M.I.T. with 291,500 shares; the exceptions were the University of Pennsylvania and Antioch College, where their respective 29,000 and 1,000 shares were voted for a student-supported proposal.

Talk about a "relevant college curriculum"! What could be more educational than for students to begin to study American corporation policy, and to get involved at stockholders' meetings by means of university proxies? For years universities have without compunction gone in for what they call field research and action programs among the poor, but when it comes to research plus action among corporations, they tend to balk. I suggest that

America's corporations are a spiritual slum, and their arrogance is the major threat to our future as a free society. There will and there should be a major struggle on the university campuses of this country on this issue.

If I go into this it means leaving the Industrial Areas Foundation after thirty years—the organization I built. What will probably happen will be that others will come forth to give full time to this campaign and that I would be with it full time for its launching and its setting out to sea. But if after what we have seen about the genesis of tactic proxy it is not clear that the genesis of Proxies for People is unpredictable, that it will develop by accidents, needs, and imagination, then both of us have wasted our time—me in recording all this and you in reading it.

Recently one of President Nixon's chief White House advisers told me, "Proxies for People would mean revolution—they'll never let you get away with it." I believe he is right that it "would mean revolution." It could mean the organization for power of a previously silent people. The way of proxy participation could mean the democratization of corporate America. It could result in the changing of their foreign operations, which would cause major shifts in national foreign policy. This could be one of the single most important breakthroughs in the revolutions of our times.

The Way Ahead

ORGANIZATION FOR ACTION will now and in the decade ahead center upon America's white middle class. That is where the power is. When more than three-fourths of our people from both the point of view of economics and of their self-identification are middle class, it is obvious that their action or inaction will determine the direction of change. Large parts of the middle class, the "silent majority," must be activated; action and articulation are one, as are silence and surrender.

We are belatedly beginning to understand this, to know that even if all the low-income parts of our population were organized—all the blacks, Mexican-Americans, Puerto Ricans, Appalachian poor whites—if through some genius of organization they were all united in a coalition, it would not be powerful enough to get significant, basic, needed changes. It would have to do what all minority organizations, small nations, labor unions, political parties or anything small, must do—seek out allies. The pragmatics of power will not allow any alternative.

The only potential allies for America's poor would be in various organized sectors of the middle class. We have seen Cesar Chavez' migrant farm workers turn to the middle class with their grape boycott. In the fight against Eastman Kodak, the blacks of Rochester, New York, turned to the middle class and their proxies.

Activists and radicals, on and off our college campuses —people who are committed to change—must make a complete turnabout. With rare exceptions, our activists and radicals are products of and rebels against our middle-class society. All rebels must attack the power states in their society. Our rebels have contemptuously rejected the values and way of life of the middle class. They have stigmatized it as materialistic, decadent, bourgeois, degenerate, imperialistic, war-mongering, brutalized, and corrupt. They are right; but we must begin from where we are if we are to build power for change, and the power and the people are in the big middle-class majority. Therefore, it is useless self-indulgence for an activist to put his past behind him. Instead, he should realize the priceless value of his middle-class experience. His middle-class identity, his familiarity with the values and problems, are invaluable for organization of his "own people." He has the background to go back, examine, and try to understand the middle-class way; now he has a compelling reason to know, for he must know if he is to organize. He must know so he can be effective in communication, tactics, creating issues and organization. He will look very differently upon his parents, their friends, and their way of life. Instead of the infantile dramatics of rejection, he will now begin to dissect and examine that way of life as he never has before. He will know that a "square" is no longer to be dismissed as such—instead, his own approach must be "square" enough to get the action started. Turning back to the middle class as an organizer, he will find that everything now has a different meaning and purpose. He learns to view actions outside of the experience of people as serving only to confuse and antagonize them. He begins to understand the differences in value definition of the older generation regarding "the privilege of college experience," and their current reaction to the tactics a sizeable minority of students uses in campus rebellions. He discovers what their definition of the police is, and their language—he discards the rhetoric that always says "pig." Instead of hostile rejection he is seeking bridges of communication and unity over the gaps, generation, value, or others. He will view with strategic sensitivity the nature of middle-class behavior with its hangups over rudeness or aggressive, insulting, profane actions. All this and more must be grasped and used to radicalize parts of the middle class.

The rough category "middle class" can be broken down into three groups: lower middle class, with incomes from $6,000 to $11,000; middle middle class, $12,000 to $20,000; and upper middle class, $20,000 to $35,000. There are marked cultural differences between the lower middle class and the rest of the middle class. In the lower middle class we encounter people who have struggled all their lives for what relatively little they have.

With a few exceptions, such as teachers, they have never gone beyond high school. They have been committed to the values of success, getting ahead, security, having their "own" home, auto, color TV, and friends. Their lives have been 90 per cent unfulfilled dreams. To escape their frustration they grasp at a last hope that their children will get that college education and realize those unfulfilled dreams. They are a fearful people, who feel threatened from all sides: the nightmare of pending retirement and old age with a Social Security decimated by inflation; the shadow of unemployment from a slumping economy, with blacks, already fearsome because the cultures conflict, threatening job competition; the high cost of long-term illness; and finally with mortgages outstanding, they dread the possibility of property devaluation from non-whites moving into their neighborhood. They are beset by taxes on incomes, food, real estate, and automobiles, at all levels—city, state, and national. Seduced by their values into installment buying, they find themselves barely able to meet long-term payments, let alone the current cost of living. Victimized by TV commercials with their fraudulent claims for food and medical products, they watch the news between the commercial with Senate committee hearings showing that the purchase of these products is largely a waste of their hard-earned money. Repeated financial crises result from accidents that they thought they were insured against only to experience the fine-print evasions of one of our most shocking confidence rackets of today, the insurance racket. Their pleasures are simple: gardening a tiny back yard behind a small house, bungalow, or ticky-tacky, in a monotonous subdivision on the fringe of suburbs; going on a Sunday drive out to the country, having a once-a-week dinner out at some place like a Howard Johnson's. Many of the so-called hard hats, police, fire, sanitation workers, schoolteachers, and much of civil service, mechanics, electricians, janitors, and semi-skilled workers are in this class.

They look at the unemployed poor as parasitical dependents, recipients of a vast variety of massive public programs all paid for by them, "the public." They see the

poor going to colleges with the waiving of admission re-
quirements and given special financial aid. In many cases
the lower middle class were denied the opportunity of
college by these very circumstances. Their bitterness is
compounded by their also paying taxes for these colleges,
for increased public services, fire, police, public health,
and welfare. They hear the poor demanding welfare as
"rights." To them this is insult on top of injury.

Seeking some meaning in life, they turn to an extreme
chauvinism and become defenders of the "American" faith.
Now they even develop rationalizations for a life of futility
and frustration. "It's the Red menace!" Now they are not
only the most vociferous in their espousal of law and order
but ripe victims for such as demagogic George Wallace,
the John Birch Society, and the Red-menace perennials.

Insecure in this fast-changing world, they cling to
illusory fixed points—which are very real to them. Even
conversation is charted toward fixing your position in the
world: "I don't want to argue with you, just tell me what
our flag means to you?" or "What do you think of those
college punks who never worked a day in their lives?"
They use revealing adjectives such as "outside agitators"
or "troublemakers" and other "When did you last beat
your wife?" questions.

On the other side they see the middle middle class
and the upper middle class assuming a liberal, democratic,
holier-than-thou position, and attacking the bigotry of the
employed poor. They see that through all kinds of tax-
evasion devices the middle middle and upper middle can
elude their share of the tax burdens—so that most of it
comes back (as they see it) upon themselves, the lower
middle class.

They see a United States Senate in which approximately one-third are millionaires and the rest with rare exception very wealthy. The bill requiring full public disclosure of senators' financial interests and prophetically titled Senate Bill 1993 (which is probably the year it will finally be passed) is "in committee," they see, and then they say to themselves, "The government represents the upper class but not us."

Many of the lower middle class are members of labor unions, churches, bowling clubs, fraternal, service, and nationality organizations. They are organizations and people that must be worked with as one would work with any other part of our population—with respect, understanding, and sympathy.

To reject them is to lose them by default. They will not shrivel and disappear. You can't switch channels and get rid of them. This is what you have been doing in your radicalized dream world but they are here and will be. If we don't win them Wallace or Spiro T. Nixon will. Never doubt it that the voice may be Agnew's but the words, the vindictive smearing, is Nixon's. There never was a vice-president who didn't either faithfully serve as his superior's faithful sounding board or else be silent.

Remember that even if you cannot win over the lower middle-class, at least parts of them must be persuaded to where there is at least communication, then to a series of partial agreements and a willingness to abstain from hard opposition as changes take place. They have their role to play in the essential prelude of reformation, in their acceptance that the ways of the past with its promises for the future no longer work and we must move ahead— where we move to may not be definite or certain, but move we must.

People must be "reformed"—so they cannot be deformed into dependency and driven through desperation to dictatorship and the death of freedom. The "silent majority," now, are hurt, bitter, suspicious, feeling rejected and at bay. This sick condition in many ways is as explosive as the current race crisis. Their fears and frustrations at their helplessness are mounting to a point of a political paranoia which can demonize people to turn to the law of survival in the narrowest sense. These emotions can go either to the far right of totalitarianism or forward to Act II of the American Revolution.

The issues of 1972 would be those of 1776, "No Taxation Without Representation." To have real representation would involve public funds being available for campaign costs so that the members of the lower middle class can campaign for political office. This can be an issue for mobilization among the lower middle class and substantial sectors of the middle middle class.

The rest of the middle class, with few exceptions, reside in suburbia, living in illusions of partial escape. Being more literate, they are even more lost. Nothing seems to make sense. They thought that a split-level house in the suburbs, two cars, two color TVs, country club membership, a bank account, children in good prep schools and then in college, and they had it made. They got it—only to discover that they didn't have it. Many have lost their children—they dropped out of sight into something called the generation gap. They have seen values they held sacred sneered at and found themselves ridiculed as squares or relics of a dead world. The frenetic scene around them is so bewildering as to induce them to either drop out into a private world, the nonexistent past, sick with its own form of social schizophrenia—or to face it and move into action. If one wants to act, the dilemma is how and where; there is no "when?" with time running out, the time is obviously now.

There are enormous basic changes ahead. We cannot continue or last in the nihilistic absurdities of our time where nothing we do makes sense. The scene around us compels us to look away quickly, if we are to cling to any sanity. We are the age of pollution, progressively burying ourselves in our own waste. We announce that our water is contaminated by our own excrement, insecticides, and detergents, and then do nothing. Even a half-witted people, if sane, would long since have done the simple and obvious—ban all detergents, develop new non-polluting insecticides, and immediately build waste-disposal units. Apparently we would rather be corpses in clean shirts. We prefer a strangling ring of dirty air to a "ring around the collar." Until the last, we'll be buried in bright white shirts. Our persistent use of our present insecticides may well ensure that the insects shall inherit the world.

Of all the pollution around us, none compares to the political pollution of the Pentagon. From a Vietnam war simultaneously suicidal and murderous to a policy of getting out by getting in deeper and wider, to the Pentagon reports that strained even a moron's intelligence that within the next six months the war would be "won," to destroying more bridges in North Vietnam than there are in the world, to counting and reporting the enemy dead from helicopters, "Okay, Joe, we've been here for fifteen minutes; let's go back and call it 150 dead," to brutalizing our younger generation with My Lais but ignoring our own principles of the Nuremberg trials, to putting our soldiers in conditions so conducive to drugs that we stand forth as freedom's liberating force of pot. This Pentagon, whose economic waste and corruption is bankrupting our nation morally as well as economically, allows Lockheed Aircraft to put one-fourth of its production in the small Georgia country town of the late Senator Russell (a powerful man in military appropriation decisions), and then transmits its appeals for federal millions to save it from its financial fiascos. Far worse is the situation in the late Representative Mendel Rivers' congressional district—he of the House Military Affairs Committee—with the phenomenal pay-offs of every kind of installation from corporations vying for Pentagon gold. Even our solid-state mental vice-president described it in a way he thought was amusing but is tragic beyond belief to any freedom-loving American.

> . . . Vice President Agnew praised Mr. Rivers for his "willingness to go to bat for the so-called and often discredited military industrial complex" as 1,150 generals, Congressmen and defense contractors applauded in the ballroom of the Washington Hilton Hotel.
> . . . Mr. Agnew said he wanted "to lay to rest the ugly, vicious, dastardly rumor" that Mr. Rivers, whose Charleston, S.C., district is chock full of military installations, "is trying to move the Pentagon piecemeal to South Carolina.
> "Even when it appeared Charleston might sink into the sea from the burden," said the Vice President, Mr. Rivers' response was, "I regret that I have but one Congressional District to my country to—I mean to give to my country."
>
> —*New York Times*, August 13, 1970

This is the Pentagon that has manufactured nearly 16,000 tons of nerve gas, why and what for being unclear except to overkill the overkill. No one has raised the questions, who got the contracts? what it cost? where the pay-offs went? Now the big question is how to dispose of it as it deteriorates and threatens to get loose among us. The Pentagon announces that the sinking of the nerve gas is safe *but from now on they will find a safe way!* The obvious American way of assuming personal responsibility for one's action is utterly ignored—otherwise, since the Pentagon made it, it should keep it, and have it all stored in the basements of the Pentagon; or, since the President as Commander-in-Chief of our armed forces believed that the sinking in the ocean of the 67 tons of nerve gas was so safe, why didn't he attest to his belief by having it dumped into the waters off San Clemente, California? Either action would at least have given some hope for the nation's future.

The record goes on without any deviations toward sanity. The army chose the final day of hearings of the President's Commission investigating the National Guard killings at Kent State, to announce that M-16 rifles would now be issued to the National Guard. The President's Commission report is doomed not to be read until after the bowl games on New Year's Day by a President who watches football on TV the afternoon of the biggest march in history on Washington, Moratorium Day. There are our generals and their "scientific" gremlins who after assurance of no radioactive menace from the atomic tests in Nevada now more than a dozen years later have sealed off 250 square miles as "contaminated with poisonous and radioactive plutonium 239." (*New York Times,* August 21, 1970.) This from the explosions in 1958! Will the "safe" disposition in 1970 of the nerve gas still be as "safe" a dozen or less years from now? One can only wonder how they will seal off some 250 miles in the Atlantic Ocean. We can assume that these same "scientific" gremlins will be assigned to the disposition of the thousands of tons of additional stockpiled nerve gas of which approximately 15,000 tons are on Okinawa and to be moved to some other island.

Compound this with a daily record of now we are in Cambodia, now we are out, now we are not in it just over it with our bombers, we will not get involved there as in Vietnam but we can't get out of Vietnam without safe-guarding Cambodia, we're doing this but really the other, with no other clue to all this madness except the half-helpful comment from the White House, "Don't listen to what we say, just watch what we do," half-helpful only because either statements or actions are sufficient to make us freeze into bewilderment and stunned disbelief. It is in such times that we are haunted by the old maxim, "Those whom the gods would destroy, they first make ludicrous."

The middle classes are numb, bewildered, scared into silence. They don't know what, if anything, they can do. This is the job for today's radical—to fan the embers of hopelessness into a flame to fight. To say, "You cannot cop out as have many of my generation!" "You cannot turn away—look at it—let us change it together!" "Look at us. We are your children. Let us not abandon each other for then we are all lost. Together we can change it for what we want. Let's start here and there—let's go!"

It is a job first of bringing hope and doing what every organizer must do with all people, all classes, places, and times—communicate the means or tactics whereby the people can feel that they have the power to do this and that and on. To a great extent the middle class of today feels more defeated and lost than do our poor.

So you return to the suburban scene of your middle

class with its variety of organizations from PTAs to League of Women Voters, consumer groups, churches, and clubs. The job is to search out the leaders in these various activities, identify their major issues, find areas of common agreement, and excite their imagination with tactics that can introduce drama and adventure into the tedium of middle-class life.

Tactics must begin within the experience of the middle class, accepting their aversion to rudeness, vulgarity, and conflict. Start them easy, don't scare them off. The opposition's reactions will provide the "education" or radicalization of the middle class. It does it every time. Tactics here, as already described, will develop in the flow of action and reaction. The chance for organization for action on pollution, inflation, Vietnam, violence, race, taxes, and other issues, is all about us. Tactics such as stock proxies and others are waiting to be hurled into the attack.

The revolution must manifest itself in the corporate sector by the corporations' realistic appraisal of conditions in the nation. The corporations must forget their nonsense about "private sectors." It is not just that government contracts and subsidies have long since blurred the line between public and private sectors, but that every American individual or corporation is public as well as private; public in that we are Americans and concerned about our national welfare. We have a double commitment and corporations had better recognize this for the sake of their own survival. Poverty, discrimination, disease, crime—everything is as much a concern of the corporation as is profits. The days when corporate public relations worked to keep the corporation out of controversy, days of playing it safe, of not offending Democratic or Republican customers, advertisers or associates—those days are done. If the same predatory drives for profits can be partially transmuted for progress, then we will have opened a whole new ball game. I suggest here that this new policy will give its executives a reason for what they are doing—a chance for a meaningful life.

A major battle will be pitched on quality and prices of consumer goods, targeting particularly on the massive misleading advertising campaigns, the costs of which are passed on to the consumer. It will be the people against Madison Avenue or "The Battle of Bunkum Hill."

Any timetable would be speculation but the writing of middle-class organization had better be on the walls by 1972.

The human cry of the second revolution is one for a meaning, a purpose for life—a cause to live for and if need be die for. Tom Paine's words, "These are the times that try men's souls," are more relevant to Part II of the American Revolution than the beginning. This is literally the revolution of the soul.

The great American dream that reached out to the stars has been lost to the stripes. We have forgotten where we came from, we don't know where we are, and we fear where we may be going. Afraid, we turn from the glorious adventure of the pursuit of happiness to a pursuit of an illusionary security in an ordered, stratified, striped society. Our way of life is symbolized to the world by the stripes of military force. At home we have made a mockery of being our brother's keeper by being his jail keeper. When Americans can no longer see the stars, the times are tragic. We must believe that it is the darkness before the dawn of a beautiful new world; we will see it when we believe it.

About the Author

SAUL ALINSKY *was born in Chicago in 1909, and educated first in the streets of that city and then in its
university. Graduate work in criminology at the University of Chicago introduced him to the Capone gang,
and later to Joliet State Prison, where he studied prison
life.*

*He founded what is known today as the Alinsky
ideology and Alinsky concepts of mass organization for
power. His work in organizing the poor to fight for their
rights as citizens has been internationally recognized. In
the late 1930's he organized the Back of the Yards area
in Chicago (Upton Sinclair's Jungle). Subsequently,
through the Industrial Areas Foundation which he began in 1940, Mr. Alinsky and his staff have helped to
organize communities not only in Chicago but throughout the country, from the black ghetto of Rochester,
New York, to the Mexican-American barrios of California. Today Mr. Alinsky's organizing attention has
turned to the middle class, and he and his associates
have a training institute for organizers. Mr. Alinsky's
early organizing efforts resulted in his being arrested
and jailed from time to time, and it was on such
occasions that he wrote most of his first book about
community organization,* Reveille for Radicals.